# A LEVEL
## Questions and Answers

D0495487

# FRENCH

**Jill Duffy**

Principal Examiner

SERIES EDITOR: BOB McDUELL

Letts
EDUCATIONAL

# Contents

# *Introduction*

## HOW TO USE THIS BOOK

The aim of this book is to help you to reach the highest possible standard in your A-or AS-level French examination (Higher Grade in Scotland). The book is designed to help all students, up to and including A grade.

The *Questions and Answers* series is based on the belief that experienced examiners can help students to achieve success by providing sample answers to examination questions, together with advice on how to deal with problems that commonly arise. Many revision aids concentrate on providing factual information – grammar, structures, vocabulary etc. – which has to be recalled during an examination. This book, while drawing attention to these points, shows how they can be used effectively to improve your standard, i.e. to **apply** your knowledge in answering examination questions.

This *Questions and Answers* book is designed to provide:

- A unit on each of the four skills of Speaking, Listening, Reading and Writing. At the beginning of each section you will find brief notes to remind you of what exactly is being tested in the examination. Those of you who are preparing for papers which combine various elements will find the individual sections useful; there is also a **Mixed Skills** unit which brings together question types involving more than one skill.

- Easy-to-use **Revision Summaries** which identify important information you need to remember if you are to achieve the highest possible standard. These summaries will give you vital hints on examination and revision technique. You should take time to read the introduction to each section before you attempt the questions or read the sample answers.

- Many examples of **examination questions**. These questions have been especially written by a Principal Examiner to reflect the actual examinations. In the Speaking unit you will find a commentary to read as you listen to the simulated oral test on the CD/cassette and in the Writing unit there is a similar commentary to read along with the **sample answers** to each type of question. The advice on essay-writing is also relevant to Coursework assignments.

- **Answers** to the Listening and Reading tasks and **Examiner's tips** on how to cope with the tasks.

- A **CD**, which provides the stimulus material you need in order to do the Listening (and some of the Mixed Skills) tasks in the book. There is also a simulated oral test on this CD: as you listen, read the examiner's comments which highlight the elements that gain high marks. The CD icon in the margin refers you to the relevant track numbers for the oral examination, listening tasks and mixed skills tasks.

## THE IMPORTANCE OF USING QUESTIONS FOR REVISION

Examination questions can help to:

- reveal gaps in your knowledge; these often become apparent only when you try to apply your knowledge to a specific task;

- increase your confidence; as you become familiar with the various types of question used, the examination paper itself will be less daunting.

## ASSESSMENT OBJECTIVES

The Assessment Objectives in French as stated by the Exam Boards are, in general terms, to demonstrate understanding of spoken and written French, and to use the language accurately for communication. The way in which these objectives are tested varies from Board to Board, but all involve the four skills of Speaking, Listening, Reading and Writing. The proportion of marks awarded to each skill also varies. Coursework may be an option, but here again the weighting given to it depends on the individual Board.

## ASSESSMENT OBJECTIVES

The examination is likely to consist of several parts. These may include some of the following, depending on the Board:

❶ A Role Play situation, for which you are given detailed instructions and which will probably be based on a sheet of stimulus material.

❷ An Interpreting exercise.

❸ Discussion of a theme suggested by stimulus material, which may be in English or in French.

❹ General conversation, leading into a discussion of topics that are likely to be of interest to an intelligent student of A-level age.

❺ Discussion of a topic prepared in advance. The topic may be literary or non-literary.

❻ Short presentation of a prepared topic.

The preparation time for the stimulus material may range from 30 minutes (the length of the previous candidate's examination) to several days. Check the requirements of your own Board.

## EXAMINATION TECHNIQUE

The oral examination is guaranteed to strike fear into the heart of all but the most confident of candidates. It is not helped by the fact that the speaking test often takes place before the written papers (though with the new modular system being adopted by many Boards this may no longer be the case). There is something about sitting in a room face to face with the examiner for half an hour that causes knees to turn to jelly, voices to wobble, and minds to become blank. Be reassured: this does not last beyond the first few minutes, and for those few minutes you are very likely to be saying something that you have prepared in advance.

The examiner knows exactly how you feel. A native speaker will have been through the French examination system that requires oral examinations to be taken in most subjects, not just in languages. An examiner who is English had to endure the same torture when he or she was taking A-level. All examiners will do their best to put you at your ease by talking to you beforehand, probably with the rest of the group.

The worst part is the time while you are waiting for your turn, perhaps as much as a day if your group is large. If you have material to prepare on the day of the examination, once you are in the preparation room you have so much to do that you have no time to be nervous. The examination itself will pass more quickly than you think, particularly if it consists of several sections. Ignore the microphone, and try to enjoy it.

As with every examination, it is a chance for you to show what you can do. There are, of course, two major differences between a speaking test and a written paper: firstly, that you meet your examiner in person (though he or she will have been instructed not to show any reaction to your mistakes) and secondly, that you do not have much opportunity to correct your errors – there is no time at the end when you can look over what you have said and put it right. Bear this in mind and don't worry if you suddenly realise that your last-but-one verb ending was wrong or that you forgot to make an adjective agree with its noun. If you realise immediately, by all means change it, but if you have gone on to something else it is not worth back-tracking; you will lose the thread of what you were saying, and that is going to lose more marks than one incorrect ending. Even to say *Pardon, je voulais dire 'attendu', non pas 'attendé'* is not worth the risk unless your train of thought is very clear in your mind.

Most Boards allocate marks in the oral examination under several headings which usually include accent, range of language, accuracy and content (not necessarily in that order of importance). You will also gain high marks if you have some original ideas to express, provided that you can back them up with evidence, and if you react well to the examiner's questions and

*Letts*
Q&A

comments. Material that is obviously pre-learned is discouraged, but examiners are reasonable people and understand that if you have prepared a topic beforehand you are bound to have learned certain phrases that you will try to use. The trick is not to sound as though you have learned them by heart.

Hesitation is a useful device. ***N'hésitez pas à hésiter****! Eh bien* at the beginning of a sentence gives you a moment – brief, certainly – to think about your answer and to take another breath. If you have in fact prepared an answer to the very question you have been asked it will stop it from sounding too 'rehearsed'. Other similar phrases – use them sparingly, but they are perfectly natural – are *Alors …, Bon, ben …,* and *euh …* (which you can lengthen into *euhhhhh …*). Do **not** say 'um'!

Don't confuse hesitation with hesitancy. If your delivery is slow and halting it will not gain many marks; this is why it is important to prepare your subject fully before you go into the examination. It would be wrong to say that candidates are marked only on the amount they say – quality is just as important, probably more important, than quantity – but it stands to reason that if you don't say much you will not score very highly.

Make sure you know exactly what you have to do in your oral examination, and how long each section of it is likely to last. You will also need to find out what your Board allows you to use in the way of notes or illustrative material, what period of preparation you are given and what you have to do in it, and whether you have to make a short presentation by way of introduction before the discussion itself.

## THE DIFFERENT ELEMENTS OF THE TEST

How can you best help yourself in each of the elements of the speaking test? There are some general points below, and you will also find more hints in the commentary on the recorded oral examination.

### Role Play

Take a few minutes of your preparation time to think yourself into your role. Decide what attitude you must take in relation to the examiner, and whether you need to use the *tu* or *vous* form of the verb.

Read through the stimulus material first, underlining or highlighting (if you are allowed to make notes during the preparation period) key points and words that are unfamiliar to you (or for which you don't know the French equivalent if the material is in English). Use your dictionary sensibly; a bilingual dictionary will give you the meanings of the words you have forgotten, but a monolingual dictionary is more likely to give you examples of the words used in context.

Think out in advance some appropriate general comments as well as deciding how you are going to convey the information required. You cannot predict exactly what the examiner will say, but the outline you are given of the part you have to play will give you some ideas.

Above all, act the part. Imagine, if you like, that you are on a stage improvising a role, and react as your character would react in the given situation.

### Interpreting

Much of the above also applies to this type of task. Remember that there will not be enough time to write down a word-for-word version of the material you are given, which anyway would not sound spontaneous.

It often happens that candidates use a different range of language in the elements for which they have had less preparation time, in comparison with topics that they have been thinking about for months. This is understandable, but need not necessarily be the case; have in mind a list of 'clever bits' – advanced structures and useful phrases that you can use when appropriate.

The examiner will be more impressed if you use them here than if you put them into your prepared discussion. Certain constructions with the subjunctive, for example, lend themselves well to Role Play and Interpretation tasks, e.g. *Je ne pense pas que ce soit le cas* – 'I don't think that's the case'.

For a list of useful constructions, see the Writing unit.

## Discussion of a theme suggested by stimulus material

## and

## General conversation

Read the newspapers, watch TV news bulletins, discuss items of interest with friends in and out of school; in English first if you wish, so that you clarify your own opinions. Then jot down in French some key vocabulary for the topic and formulate some sentences that express your views on the subject. If you are studying A-levels you are expected to know what is going on around you and to take an interest in it. Discussion is important because you need to be able to recognise more than one point of view, even if you do hold strong opinions yourself. This is also good advice for the Role Play, in which you may find yourself having to uphold a view with which you do not necessarily agree.

## Discussion of a topic prepared in advance

You will have done all the preparation for this in advance, but even so, keep up to date with your chosen topic, particularly if it is of the *'actualités'* type. During the two weeks before the recording of the simulated oral examination there was a vast amount of material in the media in France and England on both the non-literary topics. The speaking test is the one place in the French examination where you can show up-to-date knowledge of your subject.

There is a potential difficulty when you are discussing a topic you have prepared in advance; if there is something you particularly want to say it is tempting to say it regardless of what you have been asked. The oral examination is intended to be a conversation, not a monologue, so the way you respond to the examiner's questions is very important. It is just as vital to **listen** to the question in this particular part of the examination as it is to **read** the question in the written papers. If you don't understand what the examiner has said, say so or ask him or her to repeat it. It's better to do that than to give a totally irrelevant answer or flounder to a halt if you are not sure what you are talking about. The exception to this is the Role Play, in which the examiner is officially not supposed to step out of role; even so he or she is likely to help you out if you appear to be in difficulties, or to repeat the question if you have obviously misunderstood.

If the examiner asks you what seem to be really difficult questions in this section of the examination, do not despair. It may even be a good sign; he or she may have decided that you are a top-class candidate and is stretching you to see what standard you are capable of reaching.

### Notes

You may be allowed to take notes in to the examination room; in this case keep them as short as possible, and don't read at length from them. Statistics are useful; so are names and dates. For a literary topic, write down the quotations you hope to use; this is much better than taking in the text itself with bits of paper marking the appropriate pages. Leafing through a text takes time, and that means time in which you are not talking and therefore cannot be assessed. You may also lose your momentum.

### Pictures

Pictures or plans can be very helpful for certain topics, and avoid the need for long descriptions. This is particularly helpful if you are talking about a play, for example; draw and label (in French, of course) the costume you have designed for one of the characters or the set for a scene in the play. To be able to refer to a picture and explain why you have designed it in such a way is much better than trying to convey your ideas to the examiner in words alone.

**REVISION SUMMARY**

**Example of notes**

You may have to give the examiner a sheet of headings or short notes to help with the discussion. Below you will find two examples, one on a non-literary topic and one on a literary topic, to show you how you might lay these out:

*L'ordre public et la violence en France*
(Refer to Section 3 of the recorded oral test for the complete discussion on this topic.)

(a) Genres de violence qu'on voit actuellement en France
   organisée ou individuelle
   (Corse – 14 attentats mortels, 602 cas de violence en 1995)
   reportages – France-Soir  Corbeil 17/18 fév.
   'casser du flic'

(b) Causes de ces actes de violence
   récession et chômage
   l'alcool, les drogues
   violence à la télévision
   laxisme de la société

(c) La violence chez les jeunes
   Garges-les-Gonesses, maghrébin tué pour des gants
   meurtre d'un petit frère à Marseille
   l'Evénement du Jeudi – 'Enquête sur les enfants qui tuent'
   violence dans les écoles

*Antigone*
(Refer to Section 4 of the recorded oral test for the complete discussion on this topic.)

(a) Le caractère d'Antigone
   Refus du bonheur – 'un petit sourire triste' (Prologue)
   On l'admire – 'il faut faire ce que l'on peut'
   courageuse – 'Je n'aurai pas du courage éternellement'
   n'aime pas le compromis

(b) Le rôle de Créon
   roi malgré lui – 'mon rôle n'est pas bon'
   le devoir 'Pour dire oui, il faut suer et retrancher ses manches'
   mort d'Etéocle et de Polynice
   critique – Résistance, Collaboration

(c) Pour qui la tragédie est-elle la plus grande?
   Antigone elle-même – sa mort
   entraîne d'autres morts – Hémon, Eurydice
   Créon – 'condamné à vivre' – pourquoi.
   'Tu es fou, petit. Il faudrait ne jamais devenir grand'

## Presentation of a topic

If you have to give a short presentation of your chosen topic, be careful not to include in it the details that you intend to use in the discussion itself. It is better to give the reasons why you have chosen this particular subject or these particular headings. It is a chance for you to show your enthusiasm. Time carefully what you wish to say; write it out and practise it. Even though it must not sound pre-learned, it will help you to have an idea of what points you are going to make. Remember that if you do want to risk learning it by heart (and then pretending you haven't) you will probably speak more quickly in the stress of the examination, but that if you have not prepared it in detail you are likely to hesitate and therefore take longer to get through it.

**Example**

Here is a possible presentation for the *Antigone* topic (Section 4 of the recorded test):

J'ai eu l'occasion d'étudier une pièce de théâtre, *Antigone* par Jean Anouilh. Je l'ai trouvée très frappante pour deux raisons principales: d'abord parce que je m'intéresse énormément au monde classique; cette pièce est une interprétation moderne d'une pièce par Sophocle, alors en lisant les deux on peut noter les différences en ce qui concerne le traitement du thème. Deuxièmement, j'aime beaucoup les personnages, qui me semblent intéressants eux-mêmes mais qui représentent aussi quelque chose d'universel qui se trouve dans la nature humaine.

Je voudrais discuter trois sujets: le caractère d'Antigone, le rôle du roi Créon, et finalement la tragédie du dénouement.

Antigone m'attire pour plusieurs raisons. Elle est jeune – elle a presque le même âge que moi – mais moi, je ne pourrais pas faire ce qu'elle a fait. Je me suis demandé pourquoi elle a agi de cette façon, et j'ai examiné son caractère pour voir si cela peut m'aider à comprendre ses actions.

Mon deuxième sujet est le rôle de Créon. On s'imagine, n'est-ce pas, que celui qui a causé la mort de tous ceux qu'il aime serait détestable? Mais ce n'est pas le cas, parce que le spectateur éprouve plus de compassion que de haine à son égard. C'est peut-être à cause du fait qu'il a son devoir, qu'il ne veut pas faire ce qu'il a fait; je veux donc discuter son rôle pour décider dans quelle mesure cela a influencé ses actions.

Finalement j'ai voulu étudier la situation qui existe à la fin de la pièce: pour qui est-elle la plus tragique? Cette question est plus difficile à résoudre qu'on ne croit. Est-ce Antigone? – Anouilh veut peut-être que nous le pensions – ou quelqu'un d'autre? J'ai l'intention de proposer plusieurs candidats possibles.

**REVISION SUMMARY**

If you need to revise this subject more thoroughly, see the relevant topics in the *Letts* A-level *French Study Guide.*

# ORAL EXAMINATION ON CD/CASSETTE

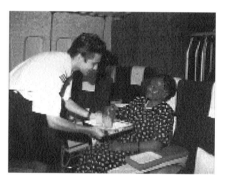

## WELCOME ON BOARD

*Air Mauritius welcomes you with pride and hopes that you will enjoy our inflight service. Our Cabin Crew will be at your disposal to make you comfortable throughout the flight and should you need any assistance or information, please do not hesitate to call them by using the call button located on the arm rest of your seat.*
*To make your journey safe and comfortable, we would like to give you some tips.*

**Hand Luggage**

For your own safety, you must place your light hand baggage either in the overhead locker or under the seat in front of you. While opening the overhead lockers, please ensure that the contents do not spill out to avoid injuries to you and your fellow passengers.

**Safety**

Watch carefully the safety demonstration and also read carefully the Safety Instruction Card placed in your seat pocket in front of you. The seat belt must be fastened for take-off and landing and when the seat belt sign is illuminated during the flight. It will be good practice to have the seat belt fastened while seated throughout the flight.

**Smoking**

Smoking is not permitted while the aircraft is on the ground or during take-off and landing, and is strictly prohibited in the aircraft toilets. Please do not smoke in the non-smoking sections and whilst standing in the Cabin.

**Seat backs and Tray tables**

Seat back must be in upright position and tray tables must be stowed for take-off and landings.

**IMPORTANT**

For your information, use of the following equipment on board is strictly prohibited and cannot be used by passengers under any circumstances:

– FM/AM/TV Transmitters or Receivers
– CD Players
– Citizens Band Transceivers
– Full Size Computer Printers
– Portable Telephones, not part of the approved aircraft installation
– Portable Video Equipment
– Remote Control Toys
– Satellite Receivers
– Scanners
– Walkie Talkies
– Wireless Microphones

A personal computer may be used on board with prior approval of the Captain, but at no time should it be used during take-off, climb, descent or the landing phase of a flight.

In general it can be said that all devices that have an Antenna OR use considerable Power OR are LASER Equipped are NOT ALLOWED.

**Inflight Entertainment**

We have provided an international selection of music and movies. Latest news is also provided on board. Please consult your copy of the Entertainment Programme on board. Headsets will be made available by the Cabin Crew free of cost after take-off. As a safety measure, please do not use the headset when the seat belt sign comes on prior to landing.

**Duty Free Boutique**

A wide variety of duty free items is available and details are available in the Boutique Brochure. Most foreign currencies and major credit cards are accepted.

**Infants and Children**

Air Mauritius prides itself in taking care of young passengers. Infant safety belts, baby bassinets, nappies, baby food and a selection of toys and games are available. Special food for babies/children can also be made available, if ordered in advance.

**Special Meals**

Special meals to conform to diet or religious requirements are available, if ordered at the time of reservation or reconfirmation of your flight.

# ROLE PLAY TASK

Look at the Role Play instructions below and read the stimulus material 'Welcome on Board',
Listen to Section 1 of the simulated oral examination. Then listen to it again, this time referring
to the Commentary.

**Candidate's instructions**

Vous êtes steward/hôtesse de l'air à bord d'un avion d'Air Mauritius. Quand les passagers
arrivent, un homme nerveux/une dame nerveuse (l'examinateur/l'examinatrice) accompagné(e)
d'un enfant, vous aborde en posant plusieurs questions qui se rapportent aux services fournis par
la compagnie. En vous référant à l'information qui se trouve sur la feuille 'Welcome on board',
répondez poliment à ses questions, essayant de le/la persuader qu'il/elle n'a rien à craindre et de
le/la convaincre de la supériorité de votre compagnie.

> **Examiner's tip** On reading the instructions you decide that you must try to calm the fears of
> the passenger, who may appear to be quite unreasonable. Your company will expect you to
> remain polite and not to laugh or show impatience, however strange the passenger's
> comments seem to be.

## Commentary

*Voyageuse: Oh pardon, Mademoiselle – Hôtesse: J'en suis sûre*

Nathalie adopts just the right tone – soothing without being patronising. She has been able to
think out her first sentence during the preparation period; bearing in mind the task that she has
been set, she can be sure that she will need to say *Ne vous inquiétez pas* at some stage during the
conversation. She has used her initiative in commenting on the weather conditions, the
excellence of which is bound to have a calming effect on the passenger's nerves.

From the point of view of language, she has used a more unusual negative (*ne ... guère* –
hardly) and a pronoun (*en* – of it), both of which will impress the examiner.

*Voyageuse: Et s'il y a un danger quelconque – Hôtesse: avant le décollage*

The examiner is enjoying herself in her role and is gently testing Nathalie to see how she will
react. A real air hostess would find it difficult not to smile at the thought of all the passengers in
the aircraft sitting in ejector seats, and might be inclined to feel impatient if asked about the
chances of survival on a routine flight; but Nathalie remains calm and soothes the examiner's
fears, using the stimulus material to help with her response (she refers to the safety
demonstration). Again she has used her initiative in mentioning the captain's years of experience
and the regular checks made on the aircraft.

Don't worry if you did not understand the examiner's second and third questions; it is
possible to answer just the first one (you should have no problem with the word *danger* because
you have been expecting to hear it, given the nature of the task). Obviously you will score more
highly if you can respond to all the parts of the question, but it is not essential to the
continuation of the task that you should do so.

Try not to drop out of your role; whereas *Je ne comprends pas* and *Voulez-vous répéter, s'il
vous plaît* are permissible in the topic discussions, they are not appropriate in this section, and
the examiner is likely to have been instructed to stay in his/her role.

Nathalie includes vocabulary that is specifically related to the topic: *le commandant de bord*,
*l'appareil* (for *l'avion*), *le décollage*. Again she chooses a more interesting negative than *ne ...
pas* (*il n'y a aucun danger*), and her use of pronouns is good (*nous allons vous montrer ...*). *Ce
qu'il faut faire* is a useful phrase which can be adapted to fit other circumstances, e.g. 'I don't
know what I should do' – *Je ne sais pas ce qu'il faut faire*.

*Voyageuse: Oh là là! – Hôtesse: Il n'y a pas de problème*

In reading the instructions for the task, Nathalie has noticed that the passenger has a child with her, so is prepared for the examiner's next question. She asks a question herself; this is an excellent move as it involves them both in a two-way exchange and does not confine the situation to an 'examiner/question, candidate/answer' routine.

Nathalie has used the most complex form of the question (*aime-t-elle jouer, a-t-elle besoin*). She could have asked *A quoi est-ce qu'elle aime jouer?* and *Elle a besoin d'un régime alimentaire spécial?*, which would have been equally correct but perhaps not quite so impressive. It is a good idea to form your questions in different ways; this will please the examiner because it shows the range of structures that you are able to use.

*Voyageuse: Quels films – Hôtesse: flashs d'information*

Warned by the stimulus material, Nathalie has prepared a film title in French. She is able to respond to the examiner's comment about the film, using the sheet of information to move the conversation along. (She would have prepared an answer to whatever reaction, favourable or unfavourable, the examiner made to the choice of film.)

> **Examiner's tip**
> It is usually a simple matter to find a film title by looking in the entertainment section or the TV guide of a French newspaper, and it is sensible to have one ready.

There is good use of vocabulary and structure. 'Flash' is acceptable here; as a general rule it is better to use a French word rather than the English or American 'borrowed' version, but in this context it is perfectly natural. *vaut la peine* ('worth it') is a phrase frequently used by the French.

> **Examiner's tip**
> Even if you know a word or phrase already it is sometimes worth checking its use in a dictionary if you are allowed to use one and if time allows. One dictionary that many students have, for example, gives the precise phrase that Nathalie has used (*il vaut la peine d'être vu*).

*Voyageuse: Bon, d'accord – Hôtesse: la monnaie de votre choix*

Nathalie would probably refer to the stimulus sheet in order to check the answer to the examiner's next question; in fact the precise information is not given, so she uses her common sense, and volunteers some additional details that are to be found on her sheet (that the passenger will be able to pay by credit card or in various currencies).

Notice Nathalie's use of the passive (*peuvent être achetées*). Chief Examiners in their comments following each year's A-level examinations often mention the fact that candidates have great difficulty with this. Don't be afraid of the passive, which is not difficult in French; revise it or ask your teacher to give you an exercise to practise if you are not sure how it works.

*Voyageuse: Bon, très bien – Hôtesse: numéros 20 et 21*

Nathalie has to be polite but firm in refusing the passenger permission to use a mobile phone, and succeeds in her task. It is worth noting that the information required to answer this question is in a separate box on the candidate's stimulus sheet; it is surprisingly easy to ignore anything that isn't in the main body of the text, so make sure that you look at everything, including headings and subheadings.

Nathalie uses a conditional tense (*ils risqueraient*). This is more interesting than the present tense, which would also make sense here. In showing the passenger to her seat, Nathalie probably hopes that she has come to the end of this section of her oral examination. She must not relax too soon, however, as the examiner still has a trick up her sleeve.

*Voyageuse: Mais c'est une section non-fumeurs! –* end

Listening to the conversation at this point we can feel sorry for Nathalie, both as an examination candidate and as the air hostess she is portraying. She remains calm, however, and her company would be proud of her. There is just a hint of reproach in her words, but she softens it with her comment *ce n'est pas grave.*

She seizes the opportunity to use a conditional perfect tense and another pronoun (*Vous auriez dû le signaler* – 'you ought to have mentioned it'). Her choice of vocabulary is masterly (*nous nous efforçons toujours de plaire à nos clients* – she has really had to put some effort into pleasing this particular customer!) and she uses complex structures, e.g. *Si vous voulez bien vous asseoir en attendant.* This time when she tries hopefully to bring the conversation to a conclusion (*Suivez-moi, je vous prie*) the examiner is satisfied.

This is a very good performance in which Nathalie has played her part well, made sensible use of the material she has been given, and included a wide range of tenses and advanced grammatical constructions. She would score very highly.

> **Examiner's tip** Look for other examples of this type of material yourself; advertisements and articles in English from magazines and newspapers are a good source.

At the end of the notes on the whole of the simulated oral examination you will find some more examples with suggested roles that you might like to practise.

Now listen to the remaining three sections of the recorded oral examination and deal with them in the same way.

For the remainder of the recorded test we are assuming that Nathalie has prepared a list of headings under which she wishes to discuss her topics (see introductory comments), and that the examiner is using them to guide the conversation. She will not, of course, use only these notes, as she will need to find out whether the candidate can respond equally well to a question that she has not previously considered.

## TOPIC DISCUSSION 1

*La situation des femmes dans le monde d'aujourd'hui*

The Role Play exercise (in which the candidate could have been a steward rather than an air hostess), and Sections 3 and 4 of this oral examination would all have been treated exactly the same for a male or female candidate. The examiner would have tackled this second section slightly differently towards the end of the discussion for a male candidate, but there is absolutely no reason why a male student should not prepare this topic.

This subject is treated in relation to the changing situation of women in the western world, not just in France, although Nathalie quite rightly refers several times to France and has chosen examples from the French media to illustrate the points she is making.

> **Examiner's tip** In choosing your topic make sure you know whether you have to relate it specifically to France (or Francophone countries). The syllabus will make it clear.

### Commentary

*Comment est-ce que la femme se voit?*

Nathalie begins by talking in general terms about the situation, making the valid point that ethnic background, age and class may make a difference to the way in which a woman sees herself. She mentions two examples of women who have reached the top of the political ladder.

(The link here is not, in fact, very strong; she might have done better to leave the examples until later and go straight on to her next comment.) She has done well to mention Switzerland; in studying A-level French you should remember that France is not the only country in which French is spoken.

These comments have the air of a presentation (see above); this is perhaps natural as the examiner has probably taken the first question from the candidate's sheet and so the answer is likely to have been practised.

It would have been easy to repeat the phrase *la situation des femmes* as in the topic title, but Nathalie shows the breadth of her vocabulary by talking this time of *la condition féminine*. Her use of pronouns is still good (*lui donnant*, which could also have been expressed as *qui lui ont donné*) and she continues to choose interesting negatives (remember that *ne ... que* means 'only').

*Et pourtant, est-ce que ce changement se reflète dans la façon dont les hommes voient les femmes?*

Here the points that Nathalie makes are well thought out and answer the question clearly: she comments that in the world of work some men now consider women to be their equals, but that their attitude may depend on their relative position in the hierarchy. She adds that many men do not adopt this attitude, which shows that she can see two sides of a question.

There is good use of vocabulary: *sensibles* (meaning 'sensitive' not 'sensible' of course), *l'attrait, vis-à-vis d'elle*.

*Et la publicité, elle vise les femmes de quelle façon?*

Nathalie is able to respond quickly to this question. She has an example ready to use to illustrate the point she is making. If she had not been asked this particular question she would probably have been able to use the quotation anyway at some stage, but in fact it fits in well here.

> **Examiner's tip** Have available several specific examples which you can use to illustrate your points. If your Board allows you to use notes, write them on a separate piece of paper or postcard; colour-code them for each topic so that you can find them easily in mid-discussion. Examples are important; they show the examiner that you have done some research into your subject.

*Sans commentaire.*

This is not a real question on the examiner's part; even so, Nathalie could have responded to it in some way.

Her example of the Renault advertisement is well-chosen, firstly because it is easily recognisable as it has attained something of a cult status, and secondly because it relates to a French product. To test her, the examiner might have asked Nathalie what the advertisement consists of, to find out if she could express herself equally well when she had not prepared in detail precisely what she wants to say. This would also give Nathalie the chance to say *il s'agit de ...*, a useful phrase meaning 'it's about ...'.

> **Examiner's tip** When you are preparing what you hope to be able to say, think out what questions the examiner is likely to ask and prepare your answers to those as well. If you are lucky you will be able to use what you have prepared, making it sound appropriately spontaneous.

*Est-ce que toutes les réclames présentent la femme d'une façon aussi péjorative?*

Again, Nathalie shows that she has been doing some detailed research into the topic. She has some precise statistics; this is always impressive, and is easy to do provided that you are allowed to refer to notes. It is difficult to keep a string of figures in your head.

Several interesting words and phrases are used here: *femmes au volant* for 'women drivers', *femmes propriétaires d'un véhicule* for 'women who own a car'. There are simpler ways of saying both these things, but again it shows Nathalie's range of vocabulary.

> **Examiner's tip** It is not always sensible to introduce English names into the discussion, simply because you may not be quite sure whether to say them as though they are French or to pronounce them in the English way. If you do this, you will have to make a conscious effort to return to your French accent afterwards.

*Donc, pourquoi est-ce que la situation des femmes a changé, selon vous?*

The examiner has moved on now to reasons why the situation has changed. It is important to be able to answer this type of question, otherwise you restrict yourself to the merely factual; higher marks are available if you are able to express your own opinions and back them up.

Nathalie again quotes statistics to support her answer; she starts off by saying *Eh bien, tout d'abord* which implies that there are other reasons she intends to give, but the examiner interrupts with a question relating to a point she has just made.

> **Examiner's tip** Be prepared to be stopped in the middle of what you are saying. The examiner's questions may be those that you have prepared, but there is a possibility that he or she may ask something you had not thought of, and you will have to think out your answer on the spot. You must respond to the precise question that is asked.

*Pourquoi cela, n'ont-elles pas les mêmes droits que les hommes?*

Nathalie continues to show an impressive amount of research into her chosen topic. Here she is using quite specific terminology for which she would probably have to refer to her notes. It would be possible to explain the laws in other terms (for example, instead of *à travail égal, salaire égal*, she could have said *ceux qui font le même travail doivent recevoir le même salaire*. When referring to the third law (which was in fact passed in 1983, not 1984, though it is unlikely that the examiner would penalise this) she could have used *il s'agit de* with a slight alteration of construction. She has succeeded in putting in a subjunctive – always a good way to gain high marks for language – in one of its less frequent uses (*quelle que soit la profession*).

Notice the first word of this answer: *si*, not *oui*. Remember that if your 'yes' is contradictory – if the questioner appeared to be expecting you to say 'no' – you need to use the stronger word.

*Et, en réalité, est-ce que le monde du travail tient compte de ces dispositions?*

In her answer to this question Nathalie makes it clear that she listens to French radio as well as reading French newspapers and magazines. There is a wealth of up-to-date material available in the media on topics such as this, and to be able to quote directly from programmes and articles is excellent. (See the introductory notes to the Listening unit for the wavelengths.)

She cleverly picks up the words used by the examiner (*tient compte de*) in the first part of her answer, using the pronoun *en* to stand for *de ces dispositions*. A simpler way to say the same thing would have been *sont obligés de le faire* ('are obliged to do so'). Another construction requiring a subjunctive is successfully used here (*bien que la maxime … soit respectée*).

*Est-ce qu'il y a des secteurs où les femmes sont moins représentées?*

Nathalie makes an interesting point here about the percentage of women in the various sectors of teaching. She ought perhaps to have made it clear that the figures she is quoting relate to France (they come, in fact, from the same radio programme that she has just mentioned).

She makes a rare mistake of pronunciation here; the 's' on the end of *univers* should not be pronounced.

*A votre avis, les femmes sont-elles contentes de leur situation actuelle?*

The examiner is asking again for the candidate's own opinions. Nathalie might have been tempted to come down firmly on one side or the other (this would have been quite acceptable provided that she could bring forward examples to support her point of view and not simply make unsupported or emotional statements), but she chooses to state that there are things to be said on both sides, and she explains the situation briefly but clearly.

**Examiner's tip** As with *alors, bon, ben* etc., a moment for thought can be gained by *Ça dépend* in answering this type of question.

Notice the construction with *permettre*: the indirect object pronoun *leur* is needed because *permettre* is followed by *à* in French. There is another type of subjunctive construction (*qu'elles soient mariées ou célibataires* – 'whether they are married or single'). *Gagne-pain* is a rare example of an idiom which means more or less the same in French as in English (it could be translated as 'breadwinner').

The examiner's last two questions in this section would have to be slightly altered for a male candidate.

*Et vous, comment envisagez-vous l'avenir, en tant que femme? Voulez-vous travailler, vous marier, avoir des enfants?*

The final questions in this section of the examination could certainly have been predicted. Nathalie, sensing no doubt that she has almost completed this section of the examination, ends with a comment that makes her own position clear.

In her answer she shows that she can express the same thing in several ways: *Je voudrais, j'ai l'intention de* and *j'espère* are all constructions that she has been able to use since GCSE but which are nevertheless perfectly valid at this level, particularly since she chooses interesting vocabulary (*concilier ma vie familiale …*).

The strength of this section of the oral examination lies in the evidence that Nathalie has assembled to support her opinions. Even though the topic did not have to be related to France alone, Nathalie has taken much of her material from French news items; the real advantage of this is that she has been able to 'borrow' many of the actual phrases used and be sure that they are correct. In this section she has succeeded in adapting the quotations she has prepared, while retaining a fairly natural tone.

## TOPIC DISCUSSION 2

*L'ordre public et la violence en France*

This topic title actually mentions the country, so you must be careful to relate the majority of your material to France itself. You may mention Britain or other countries for comparison, but you will certainly lose marks if your content is too general. Check carefully with your teacher before you start your detailed research; the syllabus may not state 'in France' in every topic title, but there may be a general instruction that 'all topics must be related directly to the country/countries concerned'.

### Commentary

*Maintenant nous allons passer au sujet de l'ordre public et la violence en France.*

As the examiner moves on to the next topic, Nathalie introduces it with a few sentences which explain that she has been following the subject recently on French radio. This shows the examiner that she has kept very much up to date with her material, and is likely to gain extra marks in the 'Content' section of the assessment.

Nathalie takes the opportunity to use yet another subjunctive construction, this time with *sans que*. *En* + present participle (*en écoutant France-Inter*) is as acceptable at A-level as it was at GCSE; if used properly (i.e. referring to the subject of the sentence) it is good style.

### *Comment se présente cette violence?*

Nathalie is ready to launch into her exposition, but the examiner interrupts her, asking for examples of the first point. She has prepared some in advance; she had probably intended to use them anyway. Although her first illustration refers to Corsica this is quite acceptable as the island is, of course, French. She consults her notes for the statistics, and her examples are particularly appropriate because she has just said that violence is seen in many different forms and the illustrations she gives do indeed relate to six different types of incident.

As before, she makes excellent use of vocabulary that is specifically related to the topic (*émeutes, saccages, attentats*). She shows that she is aware of a slang expression used in this context (*casser du flic*) and also uses a term borrowed from English (*l'hooliganisme*).

### *Comme en Angleterre.*

At this point the examiner comments on the word she has used. It is not, in fact, a question; but Nathalie could have reacted to it as if it had been, saying for example *Oui, c'est ça* or, if she were feeling really confident, *Oui; on dit en effet que l'hooliganisme a passé d'Angleterre en France*, before continuing. She says that she has chosen to concentrate on acts of violence committed by young people, and gives her reasons for doing so. This is a sensible decision, because the topic of public order and violence is vast; she is likely to gain more marks by considering fewer aspects in depth than by skimming over the surface of the whole subject.

Nathalie is confident in her use of the perfect tense of a reflexive verb (*se sont mis en grève*) and of the construction with *apprendre* (here used to mean 'teach', not 'learn'). You might think that such points are unlikely to gain much credit at A-level, but the fact remains that many candidates do make mistakes in the formation of verbs and in constructions with the infinitive. If you maintain a high standard of accuracy in using the sort of French that gained bonus marks at Higher/Extended level at GCSE, you will go some way towards a very reasonable mark for language at A-level.

### *Et à votre avis, quelles sont les causes possibles de cette violence?*

The examiner probes more deeply; she wishes to find out whether the candidate has considered the possible causes or whether she has confined herself only to the facts. Nathalie has probably been expecting this, and again has an example ready. She expresses her own opinions on the matter, relating her comments to a subject (abuse of alcohol and drugs) which is very much in the public eye at the moment.

There is good use of the passive (*un jeune maghrébin a été tué*) and of pronouns (*pour se les procurer*).

### *Avez-vous d'autres exemples de ce genre de malaise chez les jeunes?*

Nathalie is able to provide another example when asked, quoting her sources, and leading on to her next point which is a possible link between problems at home and at school.

### *C'est un cas unique, probablement.*

This time Nathalie responds to the examiner's intervention appropriately (*Non, malheureusement …*)

### *Mais ces difficultés familiales et scolaires ont toujours existé.*

The examiner decides to make things difficult for her, challenging her to agree that such problems are not new. Nathalie accepts the examiner's point, but is prepared to stand her ground; she believes that things are worse now, and cites violence on television as a possible cause.

*paraît-il* ('it seems') is a useful phrase which can be used when you are referring to something you have heard or read.

There is an error of pronunciation here – *plaignent* gained an extra syllable.

*Mais à l'école, il y a des professeurs, des surveillants chargés de la discipline. N'est-elle pas un 'sanctuaire républicain'?*

Here the examiner is really testing Nathalie, quoting from an article that she herself has read. It is perhaps too much to expect that a candidate should recognise the reference, and Nathalie could have asked for an explanation without losing ground; she might have said, for example, *Je n'ai pas entendu cette expression; qui l'a utilisé?* or *Je ne comprends pas; qu'est-ce que cela veut dire?* This would have the effect of making the examiner realise that she has pitched this particular question at too high a level; it would also allow Nathalie to take the initiative for a moment and thus relieve the pressure on herself, so that she has the opportunity to take a breath and recall the final illustrations she wishes to present.

The material she uses in her answer to this question is relevant and leads to a link being made between violence in schools and in districts where the unemployment rate is high. She goes on to distinguish between two types of violence in schools: between young people and against teachers.

She uses the expression *d'une part* ('on the one hand') to introduce one type of violence; the balance of her sentence would have been even better if she had said *d'autre part* to introduce the second element.

*Quelles sont les solutions possibles, à votre avis?*

As the examiner asks about possible solutions, Nathalie realises that this part of the discussion is almost at an end. She has, of course, been expecting this question, and has already considered what her answer will be. She makes two suggestions relating to public order, one of which refers also to a recent incident in Britain which is certainly relevant.

Nathalie has researched her vocabulary carefully, finding *îlotiers* (community policemen), *amnistie* and *remise des couteaux*. She uses the correct construction with *peut-être* (which, when followed by a verb, must either have *que* with it or have the verb and subject turned round) and has used a perfect infinitive (*semble avoir disparu* – 'seems to have disappeared').

*Et dans les écoles?*

In answering the examiner's final question in this section Nathalie mentions a solution offered by M. Bayrou, to whom she has referred in her earlier comments, and then puts forward some ideas of her own.

There are two more subjunctive constructions here, one following *a suggéré que* and the other after *il faut que*. Nathalie also uses the conditional tense (*cela leur permettrait* and *il faudrait insister*) with confidence.

If there is a criticism to be made about this section of the examination, it is that the feelings contained in it and the way in which they are expressed are almost too mature for an 18-year-old. Nathalie appears to have kept very closely to the language of the articles she has read and the programmes she has heard; the tone is therefore less natural than might be expected for a student of A-level age. The examiner might well be impressed by what the candidate has to say, provided that it is said with conviction and does not sound pre-learned. If she has reason to believe, however, that these are not Nathalie's own words (if, for example, she refers frequently to her notes or appears to be reading them) she may penalise her for lack of spontaneity. Some Boards even instruct their examiners to take away the notes if the candidate seems to be relying too heavily on them.

# LITERARY TOPIC DISCUSSION

The final section of the recorded oral examination relates to a set text. Not all Boards require
you to study literature; of those that do, some give a limited choice and some allow greater
freedom. In practice, your teacher will probably make the choice for you, or will at least offer
you the chance to study several books or plays from which you will choose the one you wish to
talk about. We have picked as an example a twentieth-century play that is popular with young
people of A-level age, *Antigone* by Jean Anouilh; the discussion ranges across several areas, an
outline of which Nathalie has prepared in advance; as before, the examiner will try to ask some
questions that she has not thought of, in order to test her ability to 'think on her feet'.

## Commentary

*Maintenant nous allons parler d'Antigone.*

At the beginning of this section Nathalie explains briefly what she likes about the play. She is
assuming that the examiner knows the plot, which may well be the case (though in the case of
Exam Boards which offer complete freedom of choice it would be unfair to expect the examiner
to be familiar with all the details of every novel or play that might be chosen). The examiner
asks her to outline briefly what happens.

Notice Nathalie's use of *dès la présentation des personnages*. She could have said *quand le
Prologue nous présente les personnages* but her construction is a little more idiomatic and
therefore likely to gain more credit. Her use of negatives (*il n'y a aucun espoir*) continues to be
good, and she is able to include present and past participles (*bravant l'interdiction de Créon* and
*amenée par les gardes*). A subjunctive construction occurs naturally, linked with a pronoun (*bien
que Créon veuille la sauver*).

*Pourquoi refuse-t-elle d'obéir?*

The examiner interrupts to make sure that Nathalie understands the reasons as well as the facts.
From the point of view of content, this is what distinguishes an oral examination that is merely
adequate from one that achieves a high mark. You must show that you understand what
motivates the characters of the play or novel you are discussing.

Here Nathalie also shows that she has studied the background of the play: she refers to the
legend on which the play is based and she obviously understands the beliefs of the ancient
Greeks.

She has clearly revised all possible uses of the subjunctive, and this time includes the phrase
*de crainte que*, remembering that it has to be followed by *ne*.

*Que pensez-vous de l'action d'Antigone?*

One of the reasons why this play is a popular choice at A-level is that it gives scope for
discussion about Antigone herself and her motives for acting as she did. This in turn can lead to

a comparison between the way of thinking of the heroes and heroines of Classical mythology and that of people in the twentieth century. It would be too simplistic to say in answer to this question *Je pense qu'elle était stupide*, and Nathalie has clearly considered Antigone's action in relation to the age in which the play is set. She also understands what motivates Antigone herself, and by using the words *refus du bonheur* she touches on one of the major themes (*le refus*) of Anouilh's work.

An important aspect of an oral examination or a topic essay is the candidate's ability to express his or her own opinions. When studying a well-known work of literature it is inevitable that you will meet certain accepted points of view, but try also to present your own interpretation of the facts; or at least choose interesting ways of expressing yourself. Nathalie does so here; she has obviously spent some time with her dictionary and has found, for example, *tenir tête à*, *inébranlable* and *lâchetés*.

> **Examiner's tip** When you are using a bilingual dictionary, first look up your word in the English–French section, then check every possibility you are given in the French–English end or (better still) in a monolingual dictionary, preferably one that gives examples. Many French words have particular shades of meaning, and you should not take the first word in the list you are given (or the one that looks most like its English equivalent) without being absolutely certain that it is the correct one.

Nathalie continues to use the subjunctive with confidence; in her answer to this question she uses it with *bien que* and with *elle craint que*. This shows the examiner that her earlier examples of it were not isolated and are therefore less likely to have been learned by heart.

*Qu'auriez-vous fait à sa place?*
This is a searching question, not so much in what it asks as in the way in which it is asked. The tense is a difficult one (a conditional perfect – 'What would you have done in her place?'. It needs to be answered in the same tense (formed, you will remember, from the conditional tense of *avoir* or *être* + the past participle): *J'aurais essayé d'oublier mon frère*. Nathalie has probably been expecting this question; she has several points to make in reply.

There is a slight mispronunciation here; the 'm' in *condamnation* should not be heard. Nathalie has got it right on the other occasions on which she uses the same word (or the verb linked to it) and it is unlikely to be penalised too severely.

> **Examiner's tip** If you are unsure how to pronounce a word, a good dictionary will usually give you a phonetic spelling. It is particularly important to check the pronunciation of words that look the same as, or very like, their English equivalents, because the temptation to pronounce them as in English is very strong.

*Que pensez-vous de Créon? Est-il le 'vilain' de la pièce, celui qui condamne sa nièce à mort pour refus d'obéissance?*

Nathalie has indicated on the list of headings that she has prepared beforehand that she wishes to discuss two characters, Antigone and Créon; the examiner now moves on to the second of these. To start with, Nathalie elaborates on what she said in her brief résumé earlier. The examiner, who clearly knows the play well, challenges Nathalie to justify Créon's actions. Her reply shows that she understands the Classical background of the play; equally impressive is her knowledge of the criticism levelled at the play at the time when it was written and the link that was perceived between the main characters and the Occupation of France.

There is good use of infinitive constructions (*il a dû renoncer à ses plaisirs* and a carefully constructed 'perhaps' clause (*peut-être aurait-il pu la rejeter*).

Nathalie uses *affermer* instead of *affermir*; an example of the fact that one letter can change the meaning of a word ('to lease' instead of 'to strengthen'). It is very easy in the stress of an oral examination to make a tiny slip of the tongue. However, taken along with the vast amount of accurate complex language and excellent pronunciation and intonation generally, it will not be harshly penalised.

*Oui, en effet, Anouilh a été critiqué par les résistants, trouvant Créon trop sympathique, et par les collaborateurs craignant l'exemple d'Antigone.*

Nathalie is not afraid to stand up to the examiner; she makes the very good point that in her opinion the characters *ont une valeur universelle* and explains what she believes this to be. She could have gone further still and added that is the essence of Classical literature (*Antigone*, of course, is a modern version of a Classical play) to consider the universal nature of mankind.

She could have acknowledged the examiner's comment briefly (*Oui, c'est vrai* before continuing *cependant …*). Her standard of language continues to be impressive; here she uses relative pronouns with confidence (*aux problèmes de la vie auxquels il ne se dérobe pas*).

*A la fin de la pièce, que pensez-vous du dénouement? Pour qui la tragédie est-elle la plus grande?*

In discussing the end of the play Nathalie responds personally (*Je suis touchée par la mort d'Antigone*) and shows that she has understood the implications of Anouilh's portrayal of events and of Antigone herself (*Elle a choisi la mort, plus par orgueil que par piété*). She again uses one of the keywords of twentieth century literature, in particular of Anouilh's plays, *refus*. She could have underlined this by stating it clearly (*Voilà, en effet, un des mots-clés de l'oeuvre d'Anouilh – le refus*).

*Et Créon?*

Nathalie has thought carefully about Créon, who on the surface appears to be, as the examiner has suggested earlier, the villain of the piece. She recognises that the tragedy is all the greater for him because he has to carry on living with his guilt; she uses the phrase *il est condamné à vivre* and explains what she means by this. (In fact the subject *Pour qui la tragédie est-elle la plus grande?* is worth a whole discussion to itself.) Her final sentence is carefully phrased to end, as she hopes, with the final picture of Créon that Anouilh gives us in the play; the examiner, doubtless appreciating this, draws the examination to a close.

There are a few mistakes in this section – one or two words are mispronounced, one of which could lead to misunderstanding if the native speaker is not feeling very sympathetic – but the overall impression that Nathalie gives is that she understands the play well and has considered its implications carefully.

## EXAM PRACTICE

Tasks A and B are two examples of the sort of stimulus material you might be given for the Role Play exercise.

Read the instructions carefully and see if you can imagine what you might say in the role you are allocated. You could also use them as Interpreting tasks.

These are not translation exercises; don't panic if you don't know a particular word from the passage. Think round it, and try to convey the sense. It will sound more natural in your own words.

# Giant jet ferry halves crossing times

**By Toby Moore**
**Transport**
**Correspondent**

A NEW generation of jet-powered ferries that will halve journey times made its debut in Britain yesterday, sailing to Dover on a day when gales delayed crossings by conventional ships.

The giant Stena High Speed Ship is powered by four gas-turbine engines developed for the Swedish air force, a horsepower equivalent to a Boeing 747.

It has a surface area equivalent to a football pitch and is five times bigger than any existing ferry.

The £65 million ship was on her way from

**Big sister: Stena HSS dwarfs a conventional ferry**

Scandinavia to begin service on the Holyhead to Dun Laoghaire crossing in March. Travellers between Ireland and Wales will be first to benefit with their 55-mile journey cut from three and a half hours to about 90 minutes.

The twin-hulled ferry carries 1,500 passengers and 375 cars. A speed of up to 50mph is twice that of a conventional roll-on, roll-off ferry.

Stena has five more catamarans on order and is likely to introduce at least one on the Dover to Calais crossing, cutting the journey time to less than 45 minutes and offering direct competition to the Channel Tunnel.

Facilities include an entertainment complex, restaurants and shops.

The company intends its fares to be a "slight premium" above a conventional crossing. However, it is offering an introductory £99 two-day return on the Holyhead route for a car and up to five people. The standard return will range from £198 to a peak of £338.

Safety features are also being stressed. There are no bow doors as all loading and unloading is via the stern.

The vehicle deck is eight metres above the water line.

Vous passez des vacances chez votre correspondant(e) français(e). En voyageant de Douvres à Calais vous avez vu le nouveau ferry dont il s'agit dans l'article ci-dessus. Discutez avec l'examinateur/l'examinatrice, qui jouera le rôle de votre correspondant(e), les avantages de ce ferry par rapport aux autres moyens de transport qu'on peut prendre pour traverser la Manche.

**Examiner's tip** If you have experience of travelling by ferry, you may well be able to use it in the course of the discussion; it will make the conversation more personal and therefore more effective.

# Fast-food France seeks return to bon appetit

## By Suzanne Lowry in Paris

THE FRENCH have gone off their food. Indeed, the *grande bouffe* that has formed part of the French lifestyle since the the time of Asterix the Gaul is over.

The baguette is disappearing. The new generation lives on frozen food, yogurt and fizzy water. It spends a rushed hour and a half at table for all three meals of the day instead of lingering over lunch alone for three hours as formerly.

What's more, traditional recipes such as *boeuf bourguignon* and *blanquette de veau* have been supplanted by interlopers: couscous is now the nation's favourite dish, rivalled only by *steak-frites*.

Such are the findings of a survey carried out for *Le Figaro*, a study which bears out the anxiety of the Minister of Agriculture, Mr Philippe Vasseur, who has just ordered a major campaign to give the nation back its "taste for taste".

Apart from television commercials there will be information kits for schools and special "tasting" events.

This should help towards what the head of the National Institute of Agronomic Research, Mr Bernard Chavassus-au-Louis has called the need for the French to relearn the "pleasure of eating".

The *Figaro* survey, which looks at how eating habits have changed over 50 years, confirms comprehensively for the first time the kind of tendencies reported individually by the bread, wine and meat industries.

Fifty years ago, an adult consumed on average 2,500 calories a day: now it is 2,000 for men and 1,800 for women, and falling.

The French have halved their consumption of bread and cut by two-thirds their potato eating. Fresh vegetable sales have fallen by a quarter and that of red meat by 15 per cent.

Cooking-oils and butter have fallen from favour by 60 per cent and sugar consumption has dropped by more than half.

Wine too has lost its nose: 90·61

litres per head in 1965, only 25·01 in 1995.

The way people eat has changed radically. The only meal that has become lengthier is breakfast: the traditional, rushed *petit dej'* of a *café creme* and (perhaps) a croissant that took an average five minutes in 1965 is now a more British or American meal with cereal and/or eggs and takes up 20 minutes.

Of most interest to the huge food industry is that the proportion of the family budget devoted to food has been slashed. In 1960 the average family devoted 35 per cent of its budget to the weekly grocery bill: today it is not more than 18 per cent.

However, the tradition of eating together round a table has not yet been eroded as it has in the "Anglo-Saxon" cultures. The French eat eight meals out of 10 at home, at table with their families. They spend less time doing it, but the ritual remains sacred.

When it comes to explaining this loss of appetite, there are plenty of reasons given: greater health-awareness, more fast food, better kitchen technology. Above all, predictably, it is a case of *cherchez la femme*.

Talk of *cuisine de grandmère* is pure nostalgia: *grandmère* these days is more likely to be running a business than sweating over a hot stove.

L'examinateur/l'examinatrice jouera le rôle du père ou de la mère de votre correspondant français. Il/elle vous dit que les Anglais ne comprennent pas que la bonne cuisine est quelque chose de très important. En vous basant sur les détails dans l'article ci-dessus, essayez de la persuader que même en France les choses peuvent changer dans ce domaine.

| **Examiner's tip** | You won't be expected to use all the details in the article above in the Role Play; read the whole passage, then choose the points that seem to you to be most interesting and also those that are most relevant to the task you have been set. |
|---|---|

**TASK C**

Listen to Section 2 of the recorded speaking test (*La situation des femmes*) and try preparing a sheet of notes for this topic.

**Examiner's tip** Work out first of all three or four general headings under which you would group the information you wish to convey, and then write down one or two sub-headings for each one (refer to the example on *L'ordre public* in the Revision Summary, if necessary). Also note down specific details – statistics, dates, quotations – that you would use.

## ASSESSMENT OBJECTIVES

The new syllabuses of the Exam Boards suggest various types of exercise that might be used in their Listening papers (or in the Listening section of a Mixed Skills unit). Some of them may be new to you; in the following pages you will find examples of most of them. Some require a 'non-verbal' response (exercises such as *Vrai/Faux*, box-ticking and matching beginnings and endings of sentences), some require words or phrases to be written in French (gap-fill, completion or correction of sentences, for example), and some are of the traditional 'question and answer' type, which you may have to complete in French or English.

Always read the instructions carefully before you start; many, if not all, of the marks available for the question may be lost if you answer in the wrong language.

Some Boards may ask you to summarise a passage in French or English. You will find some questions of this type towards the end of the CD/cassette.

### Accuracy

If you have to write in French, try to be accurate. Although it is your understanding of the passage that is being tested first and foremost, quality of language is often taken into account in at least part of the paper, so it is safer to take care with everything you write. What seems to you to be a slight spelling mistake (*moins* for *mois* or *poison* for *poisson*, or even *ou* for *où*) could lose marks because it looks like a different French word. The question that examiners ask themselves is: Would a 'sympathetic native speaker' understand this without difficulty? If the answer is no, your French will almost certainly be penalised.

(Imagine that you are reading the following sentence written in English by a French student: 'Everyone accept Paul went to the party.' At first sight it makes no sense, but when you read it aloud – not 'allowed'! – you can see what was intended. However sympathetic you are, you have had to make an effort to understand.)

## EXAMINATION TECHNIQUE

### Practice makes perfect

Many people find listening comprehension the most difficult of the four skills. The way to succeed is to practise regularly. You may think that there is little opportunity to do this on your own, but there are ways in which you can help yourself. Try tuning in to French radio; *France Inter* (162 kHz on long wave) and *Europe 1* (182 kHz) can be received quite easily in Britain, particularly at certain times of day. Listen to *Europe 1* for ten minutes at a time from just before each hour or half-hour, then again an hour later. At this time you will probably hear an advertisement or two – always a likely source for the short passages at the beginning of the paper – and the news headlines. When you listen the second time you should hear the same news stories, with perhaps some extra details added as more is known about the incident being reported. In this way you will consolidate your understanding of the news item but you will also have something more to work on. *Europe 1* broadcasts a considerable amount of pop music, often British and American as well as French, so you can practise your listening skills and enjoy the programme at the same time. You will probably find that as you hear an item for the second or third time some of the words which at first seemed incomprehensible will slot into place in your mind. *France Inter* is likely to broadcast more 'serious' material – talks and interviews, for example – so this could be useful for the sections of the paper which deal with longer passages requiring more detailed answers.

Remember that Exam Boards set their papers some time in advance, so you are unlikely to have to deal with anything that is too obviously linked to a particular date or anything that has taken place shortly before the examination.

## Comprehension hints

A wide range of test types is likely to be used, but all are intended first and foremost to test your comprehension of what you hear. It is unlikely that you will need to understand every word, but obviously certain key phrases and vocabulary will be important. If the questions on the passage are in French, you may find that they include some of the words you need; the title of the passage, if it is printed on the paper, may also be helpful. If you hear a word or phrase that you do not recognise, there is no need to panic. Try writing down an approximate spelling of the sounds you hear, then look at it as you would if you were dealing with a passage for reading comprehension. Be careful, because this may be misleading. If the words you have written down make no sense at all when you look at them, you may have misunderstood them completely; for example, *aux élus* sounds the same as *oser lu*, but in the context of the sentence *les habitants ont parlé aux élus* (or indeed in any other context) *oser lu* means nothing. The first rule of comprehension, as of translation, is that if it doesn't make sense it must be wrong. If this appears to be the case, try another spelling of the same sounds. Remember also that two phrases may sound very similar but have different meanings, both of which could make sense: e.g. *qui l'a mis* ('who put it') and *qu'il a mis* ('which he put').

## Dictionaries

The use of a dictionary is permitted by several Boards; this can be a mixed blessing in comprehension papers. You should not look on it as a reason to avoid learning vocabulary, because you will not have time to look up every word during the course of the examination. A monolingual dictionary (with definitions in French) will help you to find synonyms, and a bilingual dictionary will give you the English meanings – always supposing, of course, that you have recognised how to spell the word in the first place. Here again, a dictionary may help you as you search for all possible spellings of the sounds you hear. Think, for example, of the 'o' sound in French: it could be spelt in several different ways, including *au, eau, ot, ô, os …*

## Listening to the cassette

The greatest difference between the Exam Boards in this component is in the method used for listening. Some will give you an individual cassette which you control yourself on a personal stereo or in a language laboratory and which you can play and rewind as often as you wish within a given time. In theory this sounds wonderful. There is a danger, however, that you may spend too long on the early passages, playing and replaying in order to get the answers absolutely correct, and thus leave too little time to complete the paper. You may even discover too late that you could have answered the later passages well if only you had left enough time to deal with them. In the examination itself it is a good idea to play the whole cassette through once, filling in whatever answers you can and making a mental note of the passages that seem to you to be reasonably easy, and then go back to the beginning and deal with them in more detail.

If the cassette is played for you from the front of the examination room, this problem does not exist. Others, of course, do; there is a different type of skill involved here. The passages will have been recorded more than once, and there will be pauses on the tape to allow you to write down your answers. Use the time wisely; listen while the tape is playing, and write during the silences. You will probably not trust yourself to remember everything that you hear and will therefore feel that you have to write something down immediately; in that case you should confine yourself to brief notes or key words only. There will be time to go back and write complete sentences, if these are required, later. The important thing is to keep listening; you cannot afford to miss the next answer because you are writing while the passage is being played.

Remember that answers will usually be found in order in the passage, so if you think you have found the answers to (a) and (c) for example, (b) should be somewhere between the two; you will know the next time the passage is played exactly where to listen. 'Trigger' words will also help you; these are words that you listen for particularly because you know that when you hear them the answer you are looking for is close at hand. It is important to read the questions

carefully before you start – time is usually allowed for this if the cassette is played for you, and you must discipline yourself to do so if you are using a personal stereo or if you are in the language laboratory. Why not underline or highlight on your paper the key words in each question? Even if it is no more than 'When' or 'Where', this will remind you to listen for a phrase of time or place.

## Types of questions

Here are some general points that may help you to complete particular types of question.

### Vrai/Faux

You are unlikely to find exactly the same words used in the question as in the passage for this type of exercise; listen for synonyms, using your dictionary if you are allowed to do so.

Take particular care when the sentence is in the negative; it is natural to answer a question of this type as *faux*, but this may not be correct.

A small practical point: if you change your mind when you have written *V* or *F* (which is all that some Boards require) cross it out and write your new answer at the side. A letter that looks like a cross between the two will not be accepted.

### Gap-fill and sentence completion

Many of the answers may require the exact words that have been used in the news item. For some, however, you will need to use words which are linked to the original but may require a slight change, e.g. noun to adjective. Others may require you to show that you have understood the passage and can express the meaning without relying on the exact words of the original text. Listen carefully to the passage and check afterwards that the word you have inserted fits in grammatically.

### Gap-fill (with a list of words to choose from)

Do not attempt to complete this type of exercise without listening to the extract. You can, of course, help yourself by looking closely at the part of speech required; this will allow you to eliminate some of the words from the list each time. It is likely that there will be several words or phrases that would make sense, and only by listening to the passage will you be able to identify which particular one you should choose each time. This type of exercise often includes one or more 'distractors' – words which almost make sense but are not correct in the context.

### Matching beginnings and endings

Usually there are more endings than beginnings, so again you will have to choose carefully.

### Questions and answers (in French or English)

Answer all parts of the question. You may think that this is an unnecessary instruction, but it is surprisingly easy, particularly in the stressful atmosphere of an examination, to ignore a word or two. Marks are lost every year by candidates who, when asked 'What did Mme X do on Thursday morning, and why?' simply ignore the second part of the question.

In every type of question, look at the mark allocation that is printed beside it. A two-word answer will not be enough for three or four marks. (But be careful; if an answer is very straightforward a specific point may only be worth half a mark). The important thing is to choose the relevant information. Do not go to the other extreme and write down everything you hear in the hope that the examiner will pick out the correct information and ignore the rest. He won't; he will simply assume that you have not understood the passage, or the question, or both.

# WHAT TO REVISE FOR LISTENING

## Words that cause particular problems

In French there are certain sounds that are very similar and are therefore easily confused. Here are some words that frequently cause difficulty:

*au dessus* (above)
*au dessous* (below) – a rounder 'ou' sound.

(These two are made even more difficult to decipher by the fact that the French often 'swallow' the 'de' sound.)

*place*
*classe*

(This is a surprising one, but for some reason the combination of p or c + l is not easy to distinguish.)

*attendre* (to wait for)
*atteindre* (to reach, attain)

*étendre* (to spread out)
*éteindre* (to extinguish)

Other sounds are identical but change the function of the word in the sentence. You will remember from GCSE how easy it is to write *-é* when you mean *-er* and vice versa. It is particularly important to get this right when you are dealing with a gap-fill exercise.

*an* and *en* sound the same; bear this in mind when checking spelling in a dictionary.

A word may have two totally different meanings (e.g. *en été* – 'in summer' and *il a été* – 'he/it has been')

Don't confuse *plutôt* (rather) with *plus tôt* (earlier) – they sound alike. (See also below.)

An accent, or lack of it, can change the meaning. Look the following words up in a dictionary:

| | | | |
|---|---|---|---|
| *la côte* | *mur* | *sur* | *pâtes* |
| *à côté de* | *mûr* | *sûr* | *paté* |
| | *mûre* | | |

## Numbers

Numbers are a source of great confusion. Large numbers are often used in listening comprehension exercises, sometimes as dates and sometimes as statistics. It is tempting to ignore revision of numbers when you are studying A-level French – of course you know them, don't you? – but it is a dangerous practice. It doesn't take long to make a quick check, and it can help you to gain several marks. Look up the meaning of *mille, millier, million* and *milliard* (and if you are going to write them in figures, check how many noughts they need!). Make sure that you can hear the difference between : *deux* and *douze*

*trois, treize* and *trente*
*quatre, quatorze* and *quarante*
*cinq, quinze* and *cinquante*

Learn to distinguish quickly between the sixties and seventies, the eighties and nineties. Be careful with *vingt-quatre* and *quatre-vingts*. Get together with a friend; both make a list of numbers, read them to each other and write down what you hear. This is good practice for both of you; it improves your listening and your understanding at the same time.

Don't forget that a number may be qualified. There is a difference between *deux cents* (200) and *des centaines de* (hundreds). *-aine* can be added to *dix, douze, vingt, trente, quarante, cinquante, soixante* and *cent* to make the number more approximate (*cinquante* = 50, but *une cinquantaine de* = about 50) Other ways of doing the same thing in French include using *environ* or *à peu près*, both of which mean 'about', and *presque* (almost). Mark schemes will usually

REVISION
SUMMARY

take this into account. Watch out also for the difference between *au moins* (at least) and *moins de* (less than).

## Word combinations

Two combinations that often cause difficulty involve *cher* and *tôt*.

*très cher* = very expensive  *très tôt* = very early
*trop cher* = too expensive   *trop tôt* = too early
*plus cher* = more expensive  *plus tôt* = earlier

Some words look and sound like English words but mean something different. See the hints in the Reading unit for a list of these.

There are many more words that may create problems when you are listening to spoken French, and it would not be possible to include them all here. Make your own list. The golden rule is to learn from your mistakes; if you have mis-heard something once, make sure you check the same sound next time.

## Speed and regional accents

You will find that the speed of the French spoken in the extracts varies from one passage to another; news headlines, for example, often follow on from one another almost without a breath being taken between them, but someone making a speech will probably speak much more slowly in order to get his or her points across. Don't be surprised if the French grammar is inaccurate; after all, very few of us speak perfect English all the time, and it is just the same in other countries. Regional accents, too, can vary, and this may well be reflected in the material you hear in the examination. Some Boards state clearly that you should be studying France and Francophone (French-speaking) countries. Amongst the recorded items there is an interview with someone who has a North African accent and, at the end, an extract from a television item from Belgium.

## Questions

The questions are arranged in theory in order of difficulty; but don't worry if you find some of the early ones hard and some of the later ones easier, because many people prefer certain types of exercise and cope better with them however long and complicated the passage may be.

If there are questions on the CD/cassette of a type which your Board does not set, don't ignore them; any listening practice will help you to improve your skill.

N.B. You will find that there are two answerphone messages and a passage about the Brussels Motor Show for which there are no exercises set in this unit. The tasks for these passages are to be found in the Mixed Skills unit.

To obtain a copy of the transcript for these Listening exercises, please send a stamped, self-addressed envelope (A4) to Letts (address on inside front cover).

If you need to revise this subject more thoroughly, see the relevant topics in the *Letts* A-level *French Study Guide.*

## LISTENING TASKS

**TASK A**

Ecoutez la météo, puis décidez laquelle des trois constatations est correcte pour chaque question ci-dessous. Cochez la bonne réponse.

**1** Les températures seront

    (a) plus basses que d'habitude        ..........

    (b) plus élevées que d'habitude     ..........

    (c) les mêmes que d'habitude       ..........

**2** Dans les Alpes et dans le bassin aquitain il fera

    (a) moins nuageux qu'ailleurs       ..........

    (b) aussi nuageux qu'ailleurs        ..........

    (c) plus nuageux qu'ailleurs         ..........

**3** Dans le nord

    (a) il pleuvra à verse             ..........

    (b) il y aura des averses          ..........

    (c) il ne pleuvra pas du tout       ..........

**4** En Bretagne

    (a) le temps changera en soirée     ..........

    (b) il y aura une brise légère       ..........

    (c) il va rester calme toute la journée  ..........

**5** A l'est

    (a) il pleuvra fort              ..........

    (b) il fera beau                ..........

    (c) le ciel restera couvert presque toute la journée  ..........

**6** Dans le Midi

   (a) il fera très beau ..........

   (b) il fera mauvais ..........

   (c) il pleuvra tout le temps ..........

**7** (a) Il fera plus chaud dans le nord du pays que dans le sud

   (b) Il fera plus chaud dans le sud du pays que dans le nord ..........

   (c) Il fera plus chaud dans les régions du centre ..........

(7)

---

Décidez si les constatations suivantes sont vraies ou fausses.     V    F

**TASK B**

(a) On a enlevé le sable qui risque de causer un problème au Mont St Michel. ☐ ☐

(b) Il y a des difficultés financières en ce moment. ☐ ☐

(c) C'est une compagnie privée qui payera les frais. ☐ ☐

(d) L'abbaye ne sera pas tout à fait comme avant. ☐ ☐

(e) En ce moment le problème n'est pas très étendu. ☐ ☐

(f) La commune de Fermanville ne veut pas perdre son école. ☐ ☐

(g) Le maire est un ancien soldat. ☐ ☐

(h) Il vient de faire construire des logements supplémentaires. ☐ ☐

(i) Il y aura plus de logements pour les vieilles personnes que pour les familles. ☐ ☐

(j) On espère que chaque famille qui viendra y habiter n'aura qu'un enfant. ☐ ☐

(k) Une autre commune dans la région va détruire sa mairie. ☐ ☐

(l) On l'avait construite au début du 20e siècle. ☐ ☐

(m) Ce n'était pas très beau comme bâtiment. ☐ ☐

(n) Dans la nouvelle boutique on ne vendra que du pain. ☐ ☐

(o) On devra bâtir un nouvel hôtel de ville. ☐ ☐

(15)

**TASK C**   Remplissez les blancs avec les mots qui manquent.

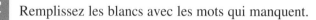

(a) Après sept ................................. consécutives l'équipe française de rugby a enfin battu

le quinze d'Angleterre. Les ........................ ont gagné le match 15–12. Le 3 février

l'équipe française jouera contre l'équipe ................................. (3)

(b) Ce soir, la suite du 24e .............................. du championnat de football. Coup d'envoi des

matchs Nice-Lens et Metz-Strasbourg à ......................... Le score du match entre Paris St

Germain et .................... a été ...................... (4)

(c) Le ........................... de l'épreuve de ski alpin qui a eu lieu hier a été Bruno Kernen, de

nationalité ................................. (2)

(d) A l'occasion des internationaux de tennis en Australie, Pete Sampras a été ...................

par un joueur classé ......................... du monde. (2)

(e) Les Palestiniens vont aux urnes pour ......................... leur Président et leurs ......................

Les élections ont lieu sous ................................................. (3)

(f) Jacques Chirac a été reçu par le ......................... C'est la première visite ...................... d'un

Président de France depuis ...................................... L'entretien a duré environ

.............................. minutes. Le Saint Père a demandé à M. Chirac de résoudre les

........................... sociales et de ........................... la famille. Des militants

antinucléaires ont ............................... près de la place S. Pierre. (7)

Ecoutez le passage. Vous trouverez ci-dessous des débuts et des fins de phrases; vous devez décider quelle fin de phrase (à droite) termine correctement chaque début de phrase (à gauche), selon le sens du passage. Il y a plus de fins que de débuts.

| 1 | 2 | 3 | 4 | 5 | 6 | 7 |
|---|---|---|---|---|---|---|
|   |   |   |   |   |   |   |

1  L'accusé doit rester incarcéré

2  Il a été mis en prison

3  Il est accusé d'être impliqué dans des actes de terrorisme

4  Il y a eu une audience

5  La prochaine audience aura lieu

6  Quant à l'audience d'extradition, Rachid n'aura des nouvelles que

7  Son avocat attend des documents

(a)  avant le 6 janvier

(b)  ce matin

(c)  trois minutes

(d)  jusqu'au début février

(e)  depuis longtemps

(f)  pendant deux mois

(g)  en été et en automne

(h)  le premier février

(i)  en novembre

(7)

Complétez les phrases ci-dessous selon le sens du texte:

(a) Certains parfums peuvent nous aider à nous ................................. le passé.  (1)

(b) Parmi les souvenirs donnés comme exemples il y a le ........................... d'une voix,

le .................... d'un gâteau et l'atmosphère d'une maison.  (2)

(c) Pour Catherine Deneuve, l'écriture de son père est évoquée par .....................................

.............................................................  (1)

(d) Elle aime les fleurs qui lui rappellent la région où elle habitait quand ...........................  (1)

(e) Elle avait l'habitude d'aller cueillir des ........................ au bord des routes de campagne.  (1)

(f) Pendant ces promenades elle se faisait souvent mal .......................................................  (1)

(g) C'est à cause de sa mère qu'elle .................................................. tant la campagne.  (1)

(h) Si on fait ce 'jeu' on ne pense plus à .............................................................................................

ou ................................................................................................................................ (2)

**TASK F**  Ecoutez les publicités. Les phrases ci-dessous ne sont pas tout à fait correctes. A vous de les corriger selon le sens de ce que vous avez entendu.

**Novotel**

(a) Imaginez que vous êtes sur la route des vacances en voiture.

.................................................................................................................................... (1)

(b) Si vous arrivez de bonne heure vous pouvez déjeuner dans le restaurant.

.................................................................................................................................

................................................................................................................................ (2)

(c) Les enfants de moins de 16 ans paient demi-tarif.

.................................................................................................................................... (1)

**Ford**

(d) Cette offre est valable à partir du 30 juin.

.................................................................................................................................... (1)

(e) La nouvelle Escort coûte seulement 71 500 francs.

.................................................................................................................................... (1)

(f) On peut profiter de n'importe quelle autre offre en même temps.

.................................................................................................................................... (1)

**Banque Sofinco**

(g) La cliente veut acheter un fauteuil neuf.

.................................................................................................................................... (1)

(h) Vous recevrez l'argent dont vous avez besoin au bout d'une semaine.

.................................................................................................................................... (1)

(i) Vous devrez fournir les détails exacts de ce que vous voulez acheter.

........................................................................................................................................ (1)

**Frolic**

(j) Le chien s'impatiente quand il est temps de sortir.

........................................................................................................................................ (1)

(k) Frolic contient seulement des céréales.

........................................................................................................................................ (1)

(l) Frolic, c'est une croquette très dure.

........................................................................................................................................ (1)

**Moulinex**

(m) La fille veut savoir si on peut laver ses vêtements.

........................................................................................................................................ (1)

(n) Le fer règle la vapeur selon la température.

........................................................................................................................................ (1)

(o) La fille est plus enthousiaste que sa mère.

........................................................................................................................................ (1)

**Air France**

(p) Concorde a fêté hier le vingtième anniversaire de ses vols commerciaux.

........................................................................................................................................ (1)

(q) Il est possible de gagner un billet pour New York.

........................................................................................................................................ (2)

(r) On pourra répondre aux questions demain, dimanche.

........................................................................................................................................ (1)

**TASK G**

**(i)** Complétez la grille avec les détails qui manquent:

| | |
|---|---|
| (a) Nombre de jours de grève qui se sont déjà écoulés | (1) |
| (b) L'heure de la réunion fixée pour aujourd'hui | (1) |
| (c) Nombre de kilomètres de ligne qui seront fermés à la suite de la signature du contrat | (1) |
| (d) Nombre d'emplois qui risquent d'être perdus | (1) |
| (e) Pourcentage des trains qu'on attend sur les grandes lignes | (1) |
| (f) Nombre de trains prévus à la Gare du Nord | (1) |
| (g) Fréquence des trains à la Gare d'Austerlitz | (1) |

Complétez les phrases suivantes selon le sens du texte, pour indiquer **quand** les choses mentionées auront (ou ont eu) lieu:

(h) Des problèmes sont prévus.................................................... à la RATP. (1)

(i) Il y aura des manifestations ............................................. contre le plan Juppé. (1)

(j) Les marins bloquaient un des bassins de Rouen ................................................ (1)

**(ii)** If your Exam Board sets questions based on a 'work' situation, you may be asked to write a summary in English of a listening text for an employer or for a colleague. Listen to Task G again, then try the following exercise:

Your employer is planning to travel to France in the next few days; he is going to Rouen and will have to go via Paris. He has heard that travelling is likely to be difficult and has asked you to find out what the situation is. You listen to the French radio and leave him a memo (in English) with the details.

..................................................................................................................

..................................................................................................................

..................................................................................................................

..................................................................................................................

..................................................................................................................

..................................................................................................................

..................................................................................................................

..................................................................................................................

.............................................................................................................. (20)

---

**(i)** Vous trouverez ci-dessous des chiffres et des définitions. A vous de décider quelle est la définition de chaque numéro. Il y a plus de définitions que de chiffres.

| 1 | 2 | 3 | 4 | 5 |
|---|---|---|---|---|
|   |   |   |   |   |

**Chiffres**

**Définitions**

**1**   presque 88 millions

(a)   habitants de Madras

**2**   420 000

(b)   enfants vaccinés par le ministre de santé

**3**   4 millions

(c)   habitants des bidonvilles de Madras

**4**   140 000

(d)   enfants visés par le programme des vaccinations

**5**   à peu près 20

(e)   enfants de moins de 5 ans qui habitent à Madras

(f)   enfants qui habitent dans les bidonvilles de Madras

(5)

**(ii)** Answer the following questions in English:

    (a) What should be the result of the vaccination programme?

       ............................................................................................................................. (3)

    (b) List the places that are being used as vaccination centres

       .............................................................................................................................

       ............................................................................................................................. (6)

    (c) How have people been told about the programme?

       ............................................................................................................................. (3)

    (d) Why is the state mentioned at the end of the report keen to participate in the vaccination programme?

       ............................................................................................................................. (2)

---

**TASK I**    Answer the following questions in English:

(a) How many people in France each year decide to do a correspondence course?

    ............................................................................................................................. (1)

(b) What are the advantages of this type of learning?

    ............................................................................................................................. (2)

(c) How do those who are following this type of course receive their lessons?

    .............................................................................................................................

    ............................................................................................................................. (3)

(d) Why have the organisations who run correspondence courses had to tighten up their procedures?

    ............................................................................................................................. (2)

(e) What conditions must be met if someone who is doing a correspondence course is to continue receiving benefits?

    .............................................................................................................................

    ............................................................................................................................. (3)

(f) How much would it cost you to obtain further information?

..................................................................................................... (1)

Répondez en français aux questions suivantes:

(a) Combien de temps les deux hommes passeront-ils dans les carrières souterraines?

..................................................................................................... (1)

(b) Que feront-ils pendant qu'ils seront là?

..................................................................................................... (1)

(c) Les carrières existent depuis quand?

..................................................................................................... (1)

(d) Qui s'est abrité là, et quand?

..................................................................................................... (2)

(e) Les deux hommes vivront à quelle profondeur?

..................................................................................................... (1)

(f) Pourquoi avaient-ils interdit la présence de leurs proches?

..................................................................................................... (1)

(g) De quoi est-ce qu'ils vont se passer?

..................................................................................................... (2)

(h) Comment est-ce qu'ils pourront se laver?

..................................................................................................... (1)

(i) Qu'est-ce qu'ils vont manger?

..................................................................................................... (2)

**TASK K**

Ecoutez le passage. Vous devez choisir dans la liste en bas un mot ou une phrase pour remplir chacun des blancs dans le résumé ci-dessous. Vous avez le droit d'utiliser chaque mot ou chaque phrase une fois seulement. Attention! Il y a plus de mots que de blancs.

| | | | |
|---|---|---|---|
| à l'occasion | après | atteindre | au début |
| composent | décider | demandent | d'ici quelques jours |
| garder | perdre | rappellent | risquent |
| sauver | sont | terminer | |

InfoMatin arrive prochainement à la fin du voyage. Ce matin, (**1**).....................d'une réunion

spécialement convoquée, on a décidé de (**2**)................ l'existence de ce journal

(**3**).......................... InfoMatin faillit (**4**).................... son deuxième anniversaire. L'avenir du

quotidien n'est pas encore certain; un administrateur doit en (**5**)...................... Dans le cas de

liquidation judiciaire les employés (**6**)................, bien sûr, d'être licenciés; mais il y a une

deuxième solution, celle du redressement judiciaire, si on pouvait trouver quelqu'un qui serait

prêt à (**7**)............. le journal. Cette solution quand même ne semble guère probable. Les

journalistes, qui (**8**)................ un peu plus de la moitié des employés, n'ont pas perdu tout espoir.

Ils se (**9**)................ bien entendu, qu'(**10**)............. InfoMatin a été populaire pour trois raisons

principales: sa formule originale, les couleurs qu'on utilisait, et son petit format.

Malheureusement cette première réussite n'a pas continué et le quotidien a fini par (**11**)...........

160 millions de francs. Un représentant du syndicat concerné dit qu'il n'est pas content de la

situation, surtout parce qu'il croit que les journaux ne (**12**)......... pas assez nombreux en France.

(12)

**TASK L**

Ecoutez le passage, puis répondez aux questions ci-dessous en français:

**1** Pourquoi est-ce que les épiciers se fâchent?

..................................................................................................................................................

.............................................................................................................................. (2)

**2** Combien de petits commerces sont touchés par les nouvelles mesures?

.............................................................................................................................. (1)

**3** Pourquoi est-ce que ces mesures ont été prises?

..................................................................................................................................................

.............................................................................................................................. (2)

**4** Comment les commerçants ont-ils réagi?

.................................................................................................. (1)

**5** Selon un des commerçants, pour qui est-ce qu'il reste ouvert le soir?

.................................................................................................. (1)

**6** Quel paradoxe y a-t-il dans cette situation, selon lui?

..............................................................................................

.................................................................................................. (2)

**7** Qu'est-ce que certains commerçants se sont résolus à faire?

..............................................................................................

.................................................................................................. (2)

You may be asked to write a summary in English of a passage you have listened to. This may have to be in note form or a continuous piece of writing (in which case you should pay particular attention to the quality of your English), and you may be given specific headings to help you with your answer.

Tasks M and N require this type of response. Listen to them carefully and play them several times; you are unlikely to be able to note down all the details at once.

If your Board is one of those that plays the cassette to the whole group, try Task M this way:

**TASK M**

**1** Play the whole passage once, then give yourself two minutes to make notes.

**2** Play it again in sections, as follows:

Section 1 - Beginning to *dialogue social*.
Section 2 - *Jacques Chirac* to *vigoureuses*.
Section 3 - *Le Président de la République* to end.

After each section allow yourself one minute to write notes. At the end allow yourself a further three minutes to finalise what you have written.

Summarise briefly in English under the following headings. You may use note form.

**1** Decision announced by Jacques Chirac at today's ceremony

.................................................................................................

.................................................................................................. (2)

**2** His hopes for 1996

..................................................................................................................................

..................................................................................................................................

.............................................................................................................. (4)

**3** What he thinks is needed in order to fulfil these dreams

..................................................................................................................................

.............................................................................................................. (4)

**4** Reaction of Marc Blondel to the President's speech

..................................................................................................................................

..................................................................................................................................

.............................................................................................................. (3)

**TASK N** Explain in English why, according to the man being interviewed, fewer people wish to buy their own home now.

..................................................................................................................................

..................................................................................................................................

..................................................................................................................................

..................................................................................................................................

..................................................................................................................................

..................................................................................................................................

..................................................................................................................................

..................................................................................................................................

..................................................................................................................................

.............................................................................................................. (10)

A summary in French may also be required. You should take care to use your own words; the whole point of the Listening and Reading papers is to test your comprehension of the French passages, and the examiners will not be convinced that you have understood if you use long sections 'lifted' from what you have heard.

If you do not have the use of a personal stereo or a language laboratory in the examination, follow the instructions for Task M as you try Task O. The sections are:

1  Beginning to *il y a de cela 20 ans* (for questions (a) and (b))
2  *Au niveau* to *refusent*
3  *Est-ce que vous avez* to *violence sexuelle* (Sections 2 and 3 are both for question (c))
4  *Pour devenir* to end.

Faites un résumé en français en vos propres termes. Utilisez les titres ci-dessous pour vous aider.  **TASK O**

(a) Situation dans les écoles à présent

.........................................................................................................................

.................................................................................................................. (2)

(b) Tâche des psychologues scolaires

.........................................................................................................................

.................................................................................................................. (2)

(c) Résumé de ce que dit le psychologue scolaire

.........................................................................................................................

.........................................................................................................................

.........................................................................................................................

.........................................................................................................................

.........................................................................................................................

.........................................................................................................................

.........................................................................................................................

.........................................................................................................................

.................................................................................................................. (8)

(d) Ce qu'il faut faire pour devenir psychologue scolaire

.............................................................................................................................................

.............................................................................................................................................

.............................................................................................................................................

.............................................................................................................................. (4)

## ASSESSMENT OBJECTIVES

The main skill that is being tested in the Reading element of the examination is your understanding of the texts. However, if you have to write any or all of your answers in French the quality of the language may also be assessed; this is certainly the case in the Mixed Skills units such as Reading and Writing, Listening and Writing and the modules such as Contemporary Society and Work and Leisure. Find out exactly what your Board's requirements are. It makes sense, of course, to write as accurately as possible anyway, because poor grammmar or incorrect spelling can make it impossible for the examiner to be sure that you have understood the text. You should read the introductory notes to the other units in this book to remind yourself of certain key points.

The level of difficulty of the French passages is likely to be varied; examination papers usually start with texts that are relatively easy, such as advertisements or short news items, and then move on to texts that are longer or more difficult (not necessarily the same thing) towards the end.

## HOW TO PREPARE

What sort of passage are you likely to have to deal with, and how can you best help yourself to prepare for this paper? The examiners assume that by this stage you are capable of understanding the sort of article that an 18-year-old French student would be reading in a newspaper or magazine. The material is also likely to be a subject that young people of that age are – or should be – interested in. So there are three ways in which you can help yourself.

❶ Read English newspapers and magazines. Not just the ones you take at home regularly; borrow different ones from your friends, so that you read a wide range of types of article in a variety of registers (formal, informal, tabloid, broadsheet, chatty, serious) and know what is going on in the world around you. This will give you a basic English vocabulary for the themes you are likely to meet in your examination paper, and you will start from a position of strength because you already understand something of the subject. It will also be a definite advantage if you have to translate into English a passage for which you already know the type of words required.

❷ Read French newspapers and magazines. These are surprisingly easy to obtain in this country, particularly during the summer months when many shops stock them for French visitors. (They are quite expensive, so why not share the cost with one or more of your French group or agree to buy them on a rota basis?) Of course, if you live in a large town or city, or in a tourist area, it is easier still, but station bookshops in smaller towns also often have them available, as do many high street bookshops.

If you go to France (or Belgium, Switzerland, Canada or North Africa) in the holidays, you can buy them for yourself; if you know that a friend or neighbour is going to a French-speaking country you can ask them to bring back for you a newspaper or magazine or some brochures from a tourist office; all of these are likely sources for examination passages.

Publications that can be bought in England include *Le Monde*, *Le Figaro* and occasionally *Libération* (newspapers), and *Elle*, *Marie-Claire*, *Marie-France* and *Paris-Match* (magazines). Look out also for the news magazines such as *L'Evénement du Jeudi*, *Le Nouvel Observateur*, *Le Point* among others.

❸ Find out whether your local or school library can obtain a CD/ROM that includes articles from the French press.

The principal advantage of regular reading of such material in French is that it creates a familiarity with the sort of vocabulary that you are likely to encounter. It would be almost impossible to make a complete list of every word you don't know, (and it would certainly take away all the enjoyment you might be feeling in reading the article) but if you find yourself coming across the same words regularly, particularly in the type of passages that appear in the main news pages, it is worth writing them down. If, when you read the passages on your examination paper, many of the words are already familiar to you, you will be much more confident and ready to deal with the particular exercise that has been set.

## EXAMINATION TECHNIQUE

The question types will probably be very similar to those you have been practising in the Listening unit (but see additional note below). It is probably fair to say, however, that the level of difficulty, particularly in the longer texts that appear towards the end of the paper, is higher in the Reading element. The very act of listening is part of the difficulty of that particular paper; you have to make an effort to understand what the words are before you can start to work out what they mean, whereas in Reading you can at least see them written down in front of you. This means that the Reading paper (or Reading element of a Mixed Skills unit), far from being the easiest way to gain marks as it was at GCSE, has now become one of the hardest, particularly if the accuracy of your written French is also being assessed.

There is an ideal way in which to deal with a reading passage, but it requires considerable self-discipline and an ability to ignore what people around you are doing. Try it when you practise some of the tasks in this unit, away from the pressure of an examination, and see whether it helps you.

❶ Read the passage from beginning to end, concentrating carefully on the meaning.

❷ Read the questions that are set on it.

❸ Read the passage again; this time, because you have read the questions, you will have a better idea of what it's about.

❹ Pick up your pen and start to answer the questions.

Tell yourself that all those people around you who are already frantically scribbling down their answers before they have had chance to read the first paragraph cannot possibly understand the text fully. This is certainly true; but in an examination the pressure to get started is so great that many candidates do just that.

## TYPES OF TESTS

The examiners' approach to testing the Reading and Listening skills is often very similar; you will find hints on how to deal with many of the possible exercise types in the introduction to the Listening unit, and others with the answers to the individual questions in this unit. There are some test types that are more likely to appear on the Reading element than the Listening.

### Explain the meaning in your own words

This is a good way for the examiner to be sure that you have understood the passage when the questions are in French. Sometimes a summary of the whole passage or of a section of it may be required, but often you are asked simply to explain a phrase or a sentence from the text. When marking such questions, the examiners will usually have identified certain elements that must be re-worded in order to show that the passage or phrase has been understood.

When a summary of the passage is required, the number of words that you may use will often be stated; this gives you some idea of how much you can leave out, although it does not help you to decide precisely what you can omit. When dealing with the re-wording of smaller sections of text, you can help yourself by practising this: take any sentence, in French or

English, and see how you think you could divide it up to explain it to someone else. Are there any words that it is impossible to put any other way? If so, there is no need to change them. To rephrase 'yesterday', for example, as 'the day before today', does not help a great deal. Use this as your criterion when deciding what needs to be altered. Usually, the section set by the examiner will be one in which most elements can be changed. Sometimes it is sufficient just to alter the construction – an adjective can be made into a phrase starting with *qui* for example – but take care that you don't simply replace each word with a synonym because the result may not reflect the meaning of the original and may also have lost its 'natural' feel because the words no longer fit so well with each other.

## Translation

Some Boards still set whole passages for formal translation, usually from French into English but occasionally the other way round. You will know if your Board does this, because it is a specific skill that you are sure to have been practising. There is no separate section for translation in this book, but several of the Reading tasks contain exercises in which translation is needed, so you can use them for practise. More frequent now is the 'transfer of meaning' type of exercise, in which you have to convey the gist of what is written but without giving a word-for-word translation of the original. In either case, there are three things to remember:

❶ Your version must reflect the meaning of the original.

❷ It must make sense.

❸ It must be written in good natural English.

All these elements are taken into account in the mark scheme.

# WHAT TO REVISE

No-one would deny that an examination is a stressful experience. Examiners setting the papers are aware of this and try to make them as pleasant and 'user-friendly' as possible. There is scope for this in the Reading paper, where the texts chosen can often be interesting or amusing and be attractive to look at, with photographs or diagrams tending to be an integral part of many questions in the new syllabuses. Because of the level of stress involved there is a risk that the candidate will make silly mistakes such as misreading a word (or, heaven forbid, an instruction) that he or she knows perfectly well. Here are some hints to help you to avoid doing this.

❶ Make sure that you know the difference between words that look very much like each other. For example:

| | |
|---|---|
| *attendre* | – to wait |
| *atteindre* | – to reach, attain |
| *entendre* | – to hear |
| *étendre* | – to extend, stretch |
| *éteindre* | – to extinguish, put out |
| *campagne* | – country or campaign |
| *compagne* | – female companion |
| *champagne* | – champagne |
| *la cour* | – yard, playground, court |
| *le cours* | – lesson |
| *les cours de tennis* | – tennis lessons |
| *les courts de tennis* | – tennis courts |
| *le fil* | – thread, wire |
| *le fils* | – son |

| *mille* | – thousand |
|---|---|
| *milles* | – miles |

There are more; keep a list of them and add to it as you come across a new one.

❷ Distinguish between words that have different meanings according to their gender:

| *le livre* | – book |
|---|---|
| *la livre* | – pound |
| *le manche* | – handle |
| *la manche* | – sleeve |
| *la Manche* | – English Channel |
| *le mode* | – way, method |
| *la mode* | – fashion |
| *le poste* | – set (radio or TV), job |
| *la Poste* | – Post Office |
| *le somme* | – nap |
| *la somme* | – sum of money |
| *le tour* | – trick, turn, trip, tour |
| *la tour* | – tower |

Again, make a list as you meet new ones.

❸ Some words are identical but have different meanings entirely. *ferme* as an adjective means 'firm', but as a noun is 'farm' and as a verb is 'close'; *été* as a noun means 'summer', but it can also be the past participle of *être*. You can probably think of more.

❹ Remember that some adjectives change their meaning according to their position. You met many of these at GCSE level: for example, *ancien, certain, cher, dernier, grand, méchant, pauvre, prochain, propre, pur, triste*. Although the English for these is usually the same whatever their position (but remember *propre* – 'own' before the noun but 'clean' after it) you will need to understand the precise meaning if you have to explain it in your own words. There's no point in saying *qui n'a pas beaucoup d'argent* to explain *pauvre* if it actually means 'poor' in the other sense. Check that you know the meanings of the adjectives in the list above (in both positions) and make a list of them.

❺ *Faux amis* or 'false friends' are words which look as though they mean one thing but in fact mean something different. You probably know many of these already; here is a reminder of some of the most useful of them:

| *actuellement* | – currently |
|---|---|
| *assister à* | – to be present at |
| *l'assistance* | – those present |
| *l'audience* | – interview, hearing |
| *l'avertissement* | – warning |
| *le car* | – coach |
| *le caractère* | – character (i.e. all the characteristics) |
| *la cave* | – cellar |
| *la conférence* | – lecture |
| *décevoir* | – to disappoint |
| *le député* | – Member of Parliament |
| *éventuel* | – possible |
| *éventuellement* | – possibly |
| *expérimenté* | – experienced |
| *l'expérience* | – can mean an experiment |

| | |
|---|---|
| *faillir* | – nearly to do something |
| *ignorer* | – not to know |
| *la lecture* | – reading |
| *la librairie* | – bookshop |
| *passer un examen* | – to take an exam |
| *rester* | – to remain |
| *sensible* | – sensitive |
| *la veste* | – jacket |

Look up in your dictionary the French for the words that those in the list above appear to mean, but don't (e.g. to assist – *aider*)

Unfortunately, the rule 'If it doesn't make sense, it must be wrong' doesn't always apply in the case of *faux amis*; they often do make sense, but they are not correct. If you come across a word that you have not met before but which looks exactly like an English word, don't jump to conclusions; it doesn't take a moment to check it in a dictionary.

**REVISION SUMMARY**

**If you need to revise this subject more thoroughly, see the relevant topics in the** *Letts* **A-level** *French Study Guide.*

## READING TASKS

Pour recevoir
votre objet
remplissez ce bon
et retournez-le
avec votre
règlement
sous enveloppe
affranchie à :

**SEVAL PID**

**37916 Tours
Cedex 9**

# UNE RADIO SANS FRONTIERE

**690 F**

Cette superbe radio
vous permettra de capter des voix et des informations du
monde entier.

Cette radio venturer multi-bandes vous offre en plus des
classiques P.O., G.O., F.M., 2 gammes d'ondes courtes,
les fréquences AIR de l'aviation civile (de 115 à 135 MHZ)
et les ondes marines (de 4 à 6 MHZ) pour capter aussi
bien des transmissions en provenance d'un avion que d'un
bateau.

Ce récepteur est muni d'une antenne gyroscopique de très
grande sensibilité et d'une antenne télescopique. Il bénéfi-
cie en plus du système AFC qui préserve la réception
même si la fréquence varie et d'un vu-mètre pour une
sélection ultra-précise des stations.
● Alimentation sur secteur (cordon fourni) ou par
   4 piles (non fournies).
● Prise micro et écouteur.
● Indicateur de charge des piles.
● Fonction ampli / porte voix.
● Livrée avec sangle de transport.
● Dimensions: 41 x 25,5 x 17,5 cm.

**Soyez à
l'écoute
du monde**

Est-ce que ces constatations sont vraies (V) ou fausses (F)?

|  |  | V | F |
|---|---|---|---|
| **1** | On peut recevoir des émissions de l'étranger. | ☐ | ☐ |
| **2** | On peut écouter des transmissions qui proviennent des avions militaires. | ☐ | ☐ |
| **3** | Une des antennes tourne pour capter les ondes. | ☐ | ☐ |
| **4** | Il y a un téléscope attaché à la radio. | ☐ | ☐ |
| **5** | La radio marche seulement si on la branche sur le courant électrique. | ☐ | ☐ |
| **6** | On peut enregistrer sa voix si on veut. | ☐ | ☐ |

**7** Pour la transporter il y a un sac spécial.  ☐ ☐

**8** Il n'est pas nécessaire de mettre un timbre sur l'enveloppe.  ☐ ☐

(8)

Lisez les petites annonces qui ont paru dans Le Soir. Est-ce que les choses ci-dessous sont nécessaires (✓) ou pas nécessaires (✗) pour les demandeurs éventuels de ces emplois?

---

**LE MINISTÈRE DES AFFAIRES SOCIALES, DE LA SANTÉ PUBLIQUE DE L'ENVIRONNEMENT**

recrute, avec contrat à durée déterminée, un

**EXPERT EN EFFET DE SERRE (m/f)**

**Fonction**: ❑ préparer et suivre les politiques et mesures sur l'effet de serre ❑ coordonner la concertation entre les administrations et les experts concernés ❑ rapporter aux instances internationales.

**Profil**: ❑ formation universitaire en sciences administratives ou environnementales et diplôme ou expérience dans l'autre domaine ❑ bonne connaissance du néerlandais.

Les candidatures, accompagnées d'un C.V. détaillé, doivent parvenir au plus tard le 15 février au **Ministère des Affaires sociales, de la Santé publique et de l'Environnement, bd Pachéco, 19, BP7, 1010 Bruxelles.**

147527 0020

**A**

---

**SGED ENCYCLOPÉDIES BORDAS**

renforcent leurs équipes de vente et recherchent pour travailler sur <u>FICHIER EXISTANT</u>

# 3 DÉLÉGUÉS COMMERCIAUX

(h/f) pour BRUXELLES et sa RÉGION

■ Ils assureront la commercialisation de produits culturels et pédagogiques ■ Débutants acceptés ■ Véhicule indispensable ■ Formation permanente ■ <u>Statut d'employé</u>

*Téléphonez au 02/534 8200 pour RDV ou envoyez C.V. + photo à S.G.E.D. (ref DC) Chaussée de Waterloo, 255 – 1060 Bruxelles*

**B**

---

**ATTENTION !**
## PROFESSIONNEIS DE LA VENTE (30-45 ans)

Nous élargissons notre réseau de diffusion pour la vente de chauffage électrique en Belgique.

Si vous êtes un vendeur capable et chevronné nous attendons votre candidature.

**Nous vous offrons**: ● une formation approfondie ● vente directe aux consommateurs ● adresses clients disponibles ● paiement hebdomadaire de la commission.
**Appelez-nous au 02-344.20.92**

142180 0020

**C**

---

# RESPONSABLE SECRETARIAT COMMERCIAL

● Maximum 35 ans
● Excel. en NL/FR/ANGL conversation, rédaction et traduction
● Expérience traitement de texte

### JOB VARIE & A RESPONSABILITES

*C.V. + photo à*:
*Huckert's International, 51, rue de la Carpe à 1080 Bruxelles*  147694 0020

**D**

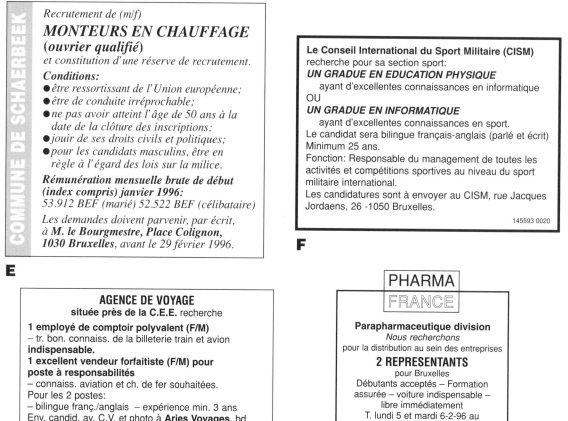

**COMMUNE DE SCHAERBEEK**

*Recrutement de (m/f)*
**MONTEURS EN CHAUFFAGE**
(**ouvrier qualifié**)
*et constitution d'une réserve de recrutement.*
**Conditions:**
● *être ressortissant de l'Union européenne;*
● *être de conduite irréprochable;*
● *ne pas avoir atteint l'âge de 50 ans à la
  date de la clôture des inscriptions;*
● *jouir de ses droits civils et politiques;*
● *pour les candidats masculins, être en
  règle à l'égard des lois sur la milice.*
**Rémunération mensuelle brute de début
(index compris) janvier 1996:**
*53.912 BEF (marié) 52.522 BEF (célibataire)*
*Les demandes doivent parvenir, par écrit,
à **M. le Bourgmestre, Place Colignon,
1030 Bruxelles**, avant le 29 février 1996.*

**E**

**Le Conseil International du Sport Militaire (CISM)**
recherche pour sa section sport:
**UN GRADUE EN EDUCATION PHYSIQUE**
   ayant d'excellentes connaissances en informatique
OU
**UN GRADUE EN INFORMATIQUE**
   ayant d'excellentes connaissances en sport.
Le candidat sera bilingue français-anglais (parlé et écrit)
Minimum 25 ans.
Fonction: Responsable du management de toutes les
activités et compétitions sportives au niveau du sport
militaire international.
Les candidatures sont à envoyer au CISM, rue Jacques
Jordaens, 26 -1050 Bruxelles.
145593 0020

**F**

**AGENCE DE VOYAGE**
**située près de la C.E.E.** recherche
**1 employé de comptoir polyvalent (F/M)**
– tr. bon. connaiss. de la billeterie train et avion
**indispensable.**
**1 excellent vendeur forfaitiste (F/M) pour
poste à responsabilités**
– connaiss. aviation et ch. de fer souhaitées.
Pour les 2 postes:
– bilingue franç./anglais – expérience min. 3 ans
Env. candid. av. C.V. et photo à **Aries Voyages,** bd
Charlemagne, 1 bte 22, 1041 Brux.          147066 0020

**G**

**PHARMA**
**FRANCE**

**Parapharmaceutique division**
*Nous recherchons*
pour la distribution au sein des entreprises
**2 REPRESENTANTS**
pour Bruxelles
Débutants acceptés – Formation
assurée – voiture indispensable –
libre immédiatement
T. lundi 5 et mardi 6-2-96 au
**041-25.11.25** hres de bureau.
139007 0020

**H**

|   |   | A | B | C | D | E | F | G | H |
|---|---|---|---|---|---|---|---|---|---|
| 1 | Expérience précédente de ce genre d'emploi | | | | | | | | |
| 2 | Connaissance de plus de deux langues | | | | | | | | |
| 3 | Connaissance en informatique | | | | | | | | |
| 4 | Age spécifié | | | | | | | | |
| 5 | Candidature écrite à la main | | | | | | | | |
| 6 | Voiture | | | | | | | | |
| 7 | Candidature reçue par une date spécifiée | | | | | | | | |

Ecrivez la lettre (**A**, **B**, **C** etc.) de l'emploi pour lequel:                                              (15)

**8**  Les produits qu'on vend seront utiles à l'enseignement.                  ..........        (1)

**9**  On doit comprendre les horaires de certains moyens de transport.        ..........        (1)

**10**  Il faut s'intéresser à l'environnement.                                 ..........        (1)

See also Mixed Skills unit.

**Letts**
**Q&A**

**(i)** Lisez les extraits du magazine Eurostar et décidez si les constatations ci-dessous se rapportent aux Belges, aux Britanniques ou aux Français. Cochez les cases appropriées.

*L*a Belgique ne s'est jamais sentie concernée par l'éternelle division de l'Europe entre le nord germanique et le sud latin. Il n'est donc pas facile de définir ce qui est "typiquement belge". D'abord parce que les Belges font tout pour être atypiques, ensuite, parce qu'on ne trouve pas plus individualistes qu'eux.

Leurs maisons en donnent un bon exemple. Tandis que leurs voisins hollandais dessinent des alignements de maisons toutes identiques, les Belges seraient horrifiés par la simple idée de cette conformité. Les Belges sont fiers de leurs maisons originales voire excentriques.

Cependant, on peut définir quelques traits typiques du Belge. Bourgeois et heureux de l'être au travail comme dans sa vie quotidienne, fier de sa maison et du bien-être de sa famille, il apprécie en connaisseur les bonnes choses de la vie et la discipline dans le travail, qui permet de se les offrir.

Les disparités entre le nord et le sud de la Belgique sont moins nombreuses et moins profondes qu'on a souvent tendance à le croire.

*I*ls aiment leur voiture et ils aiment manger. On dit souvent que les Belges préféreraient avoir un accident plutôt que de céder leur priorité. Il suffit d'ailleurs de voir le nombre élevé de voitures embouties dans Bruxelles pour le vérifier. Quand ils ne se rentrent pas dedans, les Belges sont souvent dans leur restaurant préféré. Tous les Bruxellois vous diront qu'il y a plus de restaurants primés dans le Michelin par habitant à Bruxelles qu'à Paris. On ne sait pas si c'est vrai mais vous pouvez toujours les compter.

*D*es études ont tenté d'identifier le Belge "moyen". Aujourd'hui, en particulier dans le grandes villes, il ne diffère guère de ceux qui habitent les campagnes avoisinantes. Qu'il travaille dans le public ou dans le privé, il se rend au travail avec sa voiture, et son épouse accompagne et va chercher les enfants dans sa propre voiture.

Bruxelles est petite comparée à Paris ou Londres, il est donc possible de vivre en banlieue, ou même à la campagne, et de faire des va-et-vient avec une facilité que Parisiens ou Londoniens lui envieraient sûrement.

*L*a vie dans les pubs est une institution et il n'y a pas plus grand plaisir pour les hommes que de partager quelques bières le samedi soir en déplorant les dernières performances de l'équipe locale de football ou de cricket.

La télévision: la plupart des familles la regardent chaque soir, bien que tout le monde se plaigne de l'indigence des programmes, et ce malgré le succès extraordinaire de la série récente de la BBC, "Orgueil et Préjugés" ("Pride and Prejudice").

La lecture des quotidiens populaires, pour les ragots les plus sensationnels sur les membres de la Famille Royale (sauf la Reine Mère que tout le monde aime) ou d'autre célébrités.

Passer des heures sous la pluie à dire que le temps est épouvantable.

*L*a population cosmopolite de Londres compte 7 millions de personnes (12% de la population du Royaume Uni). Il est relativement cher d'y vivre, surtout si l'on compare avec le reste de la Grande-Bretagne.

Une famille type pourrait se composer d'un père de 40 ans qui travaille dans le centre de Londres, d'une mère qui s'occupe de son bébé, et travaille peut-être à mi-temps, et d'un enfant de cinq ans qui vient d'entrer à l'école. Le père passe environ deux heures par jour dans les transports.

La principale ambition pour un couple tel que celui-ci est de rembourser son emprunt-logement qui peut dépasser largement les 100,000 £.

*L*e salarié britannique moyen travaille environ 38 heures par semaine, mais pour un cadre vivant dans une grande ville, il faut compter environ 50 heures par semaine, dues aux plus nombreuses heures de travail et à un temps plus long passé dans les transports.

Environ 44% des mères travaillent, à temps plein ou à temps partiel. La scolarité est obligatoire jusqu'à 16 ans, mais beaucoup d'enfants la poursuivent jusqu'à 18 ans; ils sont presque un million à suivre des études supérieures à plein temps.

La famille britannique moyenne dépense 12% de son revenu en emprunt-logement ou en loyer (66% sont propriétaires de leur logement, en général acheté à crédit) et 13%

dans la nourriture. Chaque année, l'Anglais moyen consomme 124 litres de bière et 17 litres de vin.

En général, une famille prend quatre semaines de vacances. La plupart des Britanniques partagent deux obsessions: le jardinage et le bricolage. On passe ses samedis à acheter les derniers kits de bricolage et ses dimanches à les monter.

*A*u pays du tertiaire, employés, cadres et professions intermédiaires représentent aujourd'hui plus de 60% de la population active. La durée hebdomadaire du temps de travail est en moyenne de 39 h. La semaine de cinq jours est une institution, mais une enquête récente montre que plus des trois quarts des salariés, en particulier les cadres, aspirent à la semaine de quatre jours.

Le salaire net moyen s'élève à environ 10 000 F. Majoritairement, les Français sont propriétaires de leur logement (54%). Paris intra muros n'abrite plus qu'un cinquième des habitants de la région parisienne.

Les dépenses d'éducation représentent 300 milliards de FF, soit 20% du budget de l'Etat. Un jeune sur deux de 16 à 25 ans est scolarisé. Six jeunes sur dix en âge d'obtenir le baccalauréat décrochent ce diplôme qui donne accès à l'enseignement supérieur (un quart des jeunes de 18 à 25 ans).

Six Français sur dix prennent des vacances l'été (trois semaines), trois sur dix l'hiver (dix jours).

*D*aniel, 42 ans, cadre commercial dans une société d'électronique et son épouse Catherine, 37 ans, infirmière, élèvent deux enfants et consacrent un quart de leurs revenus à la location de leur appartement de 75 m$^2$, dans le XVème arrondissement.

Daniel est un salarié dont les horaires dépassent allègrement le seuil légal des 39 heures. Comme beaucoup de Françaises, Catherine travaille à temps partiel. "Gain de temps que l'on peut consacrer à la famille, mais besoin d'espace: on rêve tous d'une maison avec un grand jardin, mais pour cela il faudrait s'éloigner beaucoup de Paris, car la proche banlieue n'est pas très abordable."

*Letts*
**Q&A**

|  | Belges | Britanniques | Français |
|---|---|---|---|
| (a) préfèrent des maisons qui ne se ressemblent pas |  |  |  |
| (b) passent beaucoup de temps à faire la navette |  |  |  |
| (c) aiment tout ce qui rend la vie agréable |  |  |  |
| (d) travaillent dur |  |  |  |
| (e) ont tendance à rester au collège après l'âge de 16 ans |  |  |  |
| (f) achètent leur maison au fil des années |  |  |  |
| (g) aiment faire les réparations à la maison |  |  |  |
| (h) préféreraient travailler moins |  |  |  |
| (i) à peu près un tiers part en vacances en hiver |  |  |  |
| (j) peuvent vivre à la campagne et se rendre facilement au travail à la capitale |  |  |  |
| (k) ne conduisent pas prudemment |  |  |  |
| (l) pensent que les émissions à la télé ne sont pas bonnes |  |  |  |

(13)

**(ii)** The following exercise is particularly appropriate if your Board sets 'work-related' tasks. It is based on Task C.

Votre patron vient de rentrer en Angleterre après un court séjour en Belgique. Il a l'intention d'y ouvrir une succursale de l'entreprise, mais il ne sait pas beaucoup à propos des Belges. Il vous demande de faire un résumé en anglais des points principaux des paragraphes à leur sujet qu'il a trouvés dans le magazine d'Eurostar.

According to the magazine, the Belgians...................................................................................

........................................................................................................................................

........................................................................................................................................

........................................................................................................................................

........................................................................................................................................

........................................................................................................................................

........................................................................................................................................

..............................................................................................................................

..............................................................................................................................

..............................................................................................................................

..............................................................................................................................

..............................................................................................................................

..............................................................................................................................

..............................................................................................................................

..............................................................................................................................

..............................................................................................................................

..............................................................................................................................

.................................................................................................................... (20)

## *Grèves*

Il est nécessaire de tirer l'enseignement des événements déclenchés par une poignée d'hommes qui paralysent et appauvrissent la France.

1) Il existe en France un contre-pouvoir, composé de syndicats, minoritaires en nombre, mais très organisés dans les techniques de désorganisation, et qui refusent la démocratie.

**A**

2) Les syndicats ne représentent pas les « travailleurs », puisque moins de 10% de ces derniers y sont affiliés.

3) Les syndicats ne défendent pas les intérêts de tous les « travailleurs », puisqu'ils infligent á la majorité d'entre eux un lot de difficultés, en mobilisant une minorité avec de fallacieux prétextes.

4) En conclusion, le système syndical français ressemble, non à la « dictature du prolétariat », mais à celle de ses dirigeants, et c'est pourquoi il est nécessaire de le réformer d'urgence, en le remplaçant par des syndicats professionnels (comme chez nos voisins), non politiques.

## *Mitterrand*

Le médecin personnel du défunt président de la République confirme que celui-ci était bien atteint d'un cancer dès sa première élection. Il a tort, j'en conviens, et devrait respecter le secret médical. Mais il a eu encore plus tort de délivrer ou faire délivrer des certificats médicaux mensongers, répétés pendant plus de onze ans. Et, sur France-Inter, le président du Conseil de l'Ordre ne s'indigne que de la transgression du secret médical. La délivrance de certificats médicaux contraires à la vérité ne semble absolument pas le choquer. Qui pourra désormais blâmer le salarié moyen qui, pour prendre huit jours d'arrêt de travail, demandera un certificat de complaisance à son médecin, ou le médecln qui délivrera un tel certificat?

**B**

**C** Les patrons des syndicats poussent les salariés à des grèves dévastatrices. Quand on sait que les leaders syndicaux sont des agents du PS et du PC, on peut s'interroger sur la responsabilité de ces partis, et surtout du PS, dans le déclenchement et la poursuite des grèves. Il est, en tout cas, anormal que les patrons du PS, qui se prétendent aptes à gouverner, ne dénoncent pas des mouvements qui risquent de déstabiliser les entreprises et d'aggraver le chômage.

### Gardes-chasse

**D** Ces 1,6 million porteurs de fusils monopolisent, envahissent et disposent d'un territoire sur lequel évoluent plus de cinquante millions d'humains et quelques milliards d'animaux. La balance est faussée et ce sont ces 3% qui font la loi et occupent périodiquement le territoire national. De cette occupation, les animaux sont toujours les victimes et les humains quelquefois. Il est urgent d'instaurer une réelle garderie nationale de l'environnement, qui ne soit plus placée sous la dépendance des fédérations départementales de chasseurs. 1 600 gardes ne pèsent pas lourd dans la balance politique, mais comparativement, ils sont au moins aussi victimes que les personnels de police ou de gendarmerie.

### Clovis

**E** Il y a beaucoup de choses intéressantes dans l'article de J.-L. Nothias « *Clovis, le premier Parisien* (Figaro *du 15 janvier*). Il en manque pourtant.
  1. La date. C'est en 508, au retour de sa conquête de l'Aquitaine, que Clovis choisit Paris pour résidence.
  2. Le lieu. A la place de l'actuel palais de justice, dans l'île de la Cité, où s'élevaient les restes du palais édifié par Constance Chlore et son successeur Julien.
  3. L'une des principales raisons : situation au centre, non seulement de son nouveau royaume, mais des villas royales qui entretenaient son train de maison : Clichy au nord, Chelles à l'est, Bonneuil au sud-est, Ruell à l'ouest.

**F** La prise en otage de soixante millions d'usagers par les agents des transports et de la Poste est un abus qui relève du fascisme. Il serait temps :
– pour ces usagers de se montrer aussi dans la rue pour protester;
– pour la télévision de tenir la part égale dans le débat;
– enfin, pour le gouvernement, de prendre une attitude offensive, en attaquant les irresponsables qui veulent le torpillage de tout plan pouvant sortir notre économie du marasme.

Vous trouverez ci-dessus et à la page précédente des lettres qui ont paru dans *Le Figaro*. Décidez quelle phrase explique le mieux l'attitude de celui/celle qui a écrit chaque lettre.

1  trouve que la déontologie a été violée                                    ..........

2  croit qu'on devrait établir un système de protection plus efficace         ..........

3  pense que certains détails importants avaient été omis de l'article d'un
   numéro précédent                                                          ..........

4  affirme que l'influence d'une minorité de gens est trop grande           ..........

5  fait voir sa colère                                                       ..........

6  mettent les problèmes sur le compte des trublions politiques             ..........

(6)

# La magie des rencontres

# EXPLORATOR
## VOYAGES – EXPEDITIONS

Emotion des rencontres, beauté des paysages, richesse des civilisations. EXPLORATOR vous offre ce rare équilibre entre les hommes, la nature et les sites. 120 itinéraires à travers le monde, dans 60 pays, pour vivre des instants uniques. La connaissance du terrain et la maîtrise de l'organisation permettent à EXPLORATOR de vous éviter tout effort physique particulier et d'assurer le parfait déroulement de votre expédition ou de votre voyage.

Demandez notre brochure, nous vous l'enverrons gracieusement : vous y trouverez votre prochain et plus beau voyage.

**EXPLORATOR
La passion
de la découverte**

## DEMANDE DE BROCHURE
*MERCI D'ÉCRIRE TRÈS LISIBLEMENT*

NOM                                        PRENOM

ADRESSE

                                           TEL

DESIRE RECEVOIR LA BROCHURE EXPLORATOR

EXPLORATOR - 16, place de la Madeleine, 75008 Paris
Tél. (1) 42.66.66.24. **Minitel 3615 EXPLO**

This is a simple language-manipulation exercise to get you into the habit of expressing things in your own words.

In the first six questions, all you have to do is to change the part of speech (noun, verb, adjective etc.) in the passage to one that will fit properly into the sentence you are given.

(a) Vous verrez de ................................... paysages. (1)

(b) Les voyages qu'Explorator vous offre sont bien ............................ entre les
   hommes, la nature et les sites. (1)

(c) Explorator ....................................... bien le terrain des expéditions. (1)

(d) Votre expédition ......................................... parfaitement. (1)

(e) La brochure vous sera ................................. gracieusement. (1)

(f) Il faut remplir le coupon en écrivant d'une façon ................................. (1)

In the next three sentences you will have to find the part of the text to which the sentence refers and decide how you can express its meaning using the framework of the sentence you have been given. This will probably mean moving a little further away from the original text.

(g) Vous pourrez vivre des instants qui .................................................... (1)

(h) Aucun effort physique particulier ...................................................... (1)

(i) Vous trouverez ......................................... votre prochain et plus beau voyage. (1)

See also the Mixed Skills unit.

**(i)** Remplissez la grille avec les détails nécessaires; pas besoin d'écrire des phrases complètes. Vous trouverez les réponses dans les trois premiers paragraphes du texte.

---

## Nouvel assassinat d'un militant nationaliste en Corse

LA « *GUERRE CIVILE* » entre nationalistes corses a-t-elle repris, vendredi 16 février, dans les rues d'Ajaccio ? C'est désormais la question qui se pose après la mort de Jules Massa âgé de quarante et un ans, garde du corps de François Santoni, souvent présenté comme l'un des dirigeants du FLNC-canal historique. Jules Massa a été tué de plusieurs balles devant une école du quartier des Salines, à l'entrée sud d'Ajaccio.

En 1995, onze militants nationalistes ont été tués dans des assassinats restés inexpliqués, où se mêlaient vengeances personnelles, rivalités politiques et sans doute, pour certains, règlements de compte relevant du droit commun. François Santoni lui-même avait été grièvement blessé le 29 mai 1995, lors d'un attentat où le garde du corps qui l'accompagnait, Stéphane Gallo, avait été tué. Quelques jours auparavant, le 19 mai, Jules Massa avait été arrêté pour port d'armes prohibé et condamné à six mois de prison, dont quatre avec sursis, ce qui lui avait peut-être sauvé la vie...

Le dernier assassinat date du 28 octobre 1995. Un meurtre, dans la nuit du nouvel An, avait pu laisser penser que la guerre s'était rallumée. Mais les enquêteurs se sont orientés vers d'autres pistes. A l'automne, des négociations – impliquant des personnalités extérieures à la mouvance nationaliste – avaient abouti à une sorte de paix armée. Cet assassinat pose aussi un nouveau problème au gouvernement et à Jean-Louis Debré, le ministre de l'intérieur, responsable du dossier corse et engagé dans un dialogue avec l'ensemble des composantes politiques, y compris les nationalistes. De l'avis général en effet, une conjonction de facteurs offrait une ouverture politique peut-être exceptionnelle. Ce nouveau climat a été symbolisé par l'annonce, en janvier, d'une trêve des attentats du FLNC-canal historique.

Le 16 février est la date anniversaire de l'assassinat de Jean-Pierre Leca, garde du corps d'Alain Orsoni, dirigeant du MPA. Cet assassinat n'a jamais été revendiqué par le FLNC-canal historique et est plutôt attribué à un règlement de comptes commandité par le Milieu. De source proche du FLNC-canal historique, on estimait vendredi matin que le nouvel assassinat était sans doute à mettre au compte des « *contentieux personnels* », et ne remet pas en cause le processus politique en cours.

De fait, les dirigeants de la *Cuncolta*, vitrine légale du FLNC-canal historique ne cessent de souligner leur attachement à ce processus. Un nouveau pas devait être franchi samedi avec la transformation de la *Cuncolta* en parti politique avec François Santoni, précisément, comme l'un des dirigeants.

*J.-L. A.*

---

| | |
|---|---|
| (a) Détails du décédé | (2) |
| (b) Méthode de l'assassinat | (1) |
| (c) Lieu du crime | (3) |
| (d) Raisons éventuelles des meurtres en 1995 | (3) |
| (e) Sentence prononcée contre Jules Massa en mai 1995 | (2) |
| (f) Ce que le ministre de l'intérieur est en train de faire | (2) |
| (g) Preuve d'une amélioration éventuelle de la situation | (2) |

**(ii)** Reformulez les phrases suivantes en utilisant la forme correcte du mot entre parenthèses. Les phrases sont prises dans les deux derniers paragraphes du texte.

(a) (TUÉ) Le 16 février est la date anniversaire de l'assassinat de Jean-Pierre Leca

........................................................................................................................

................................................................................................................ (2)

(b) (CULPABILITÉ) Cet assassinat n'a jamais été revendiqué par le FLNC-canal historique

........................................................................................................................

................................................................................................................ (2)

(c) (TRAIN) Le processus politique en cours

................................................................................................................ (1)

(d) (CEUX) Les dirigeants de la Cuncolta

................................................................................................................ (2)

(e) (ON) Un nouveau pas devait être franchi

................................................................................................................ (2)

## CINEMA
### PHÉNOMÈNE

Depuis trente-cinq ans, il est le plus célèbre des Gaulois, après Vercingétorix. Avec le nouveau dessin animé long métrage contant ses aventures outre-Atlantique, « Astérix et les Indiens » qui vient de sortir, l' « astérixmania » n'est pas près de faiblir. Bilan.

« *Astérix et les Indiens* ».

# Astérix résiste encore et toujours!

Été 1959. René Goscinny et Albert Uderzo, qui avaient commencé huit ans plus tôt une fertile collaboration, se creusent les méninges à la recherche d'un nouveau personnage de BD. Toutatis, Belenos et les autres dieux du panthéon gaulois veillent sans doute à leur inspiration puisque, le 29 octobre suivant, apparaissent pour la première fois, dans *Pilote*, les moustaches jaunes d'Astérix. Une légende vient de naître que la disparition de Goscinny, en 1977, n'entamera pas. Depuis *Astérix le Gaulois*, paru chez Dargaud en 1961, jusqu'à *la Rose et le Glaive*, dont la publication a fait grand bruit (7 millions d'albums mis en place dans toute l'Europe, le 18 octobre 1991), plus de 260 millions d'albums se sont vendus, traduits en 57 langues et dialectes! Phénomène d'édition, le petit Gaulois ne tarde pas à devenir une star à part entière, suscitant bien des hommages. Le premier satellite français lancé dans l'espace, en 1965, est ainsi baptisé Astérix. Un an plus tard, *l'Express* n'hésite pas à lui consacrer sa « une ». En 1988, alors que Jérôme Savary donne chair et os à Astérix dans un spectacle représenté au Cirque d'hiver, un service télématique (qui fonctionne toujours) lui est dédié, proposant jeux et informations à ses fidèles. Il suffit de taper 36 15 ASTERIX, bien sûr. Enfin, honneur suprême, pour illustrer un dossier intitulé « The New France », le magazine *Time* accorde sa couverture, en 1991, à celui qu'un sondage Sofres sacre chez nous personnage le plus populaire de la bande dessinée, avant Tintin, Mickey et Lucky Luke!

Parallèlement, l'astérixmania déferle, avec une colossale opération de merchandising propre à enflammer la fièvre collectionneuse des aficionados comme Marc Jallon, qui a dévoilé ses 5 000 pièces au public dans un ouvrage intitulé *Toutastérix* (1). Dès 1963, les licences d'exploitation se sont en effet multipliées, permettant à des centaines de firmes d'utiliser le personnage dessiné par Goscinny pour fabriquer des objets à son effigie (figurines, stylos, cendriers, tee-shirts, pin's...) ou promouvoir des produits aussi divers que savons, biscuits, fromages, lessives, essence... Au risque de connaître des dérapages. Depuis 1982, les éditions Albert René, créées en 1979 à la suite d'un différend avec Dargaud, détiennent les droits mondiaux de l'univers d'Astérix.

Cet incroyable engouement ne pouvait manquer d'intéresser l'industrie du septième art. Premier dessin animé, *Astérix le Gaulois* fait un véritable tabac en 1967, pulvérisant même les records détenus par Disney en Allemagne, où le héros de Goscinny et Uderzo est presque aussi célèbre que chez lui (82 millions d'albums vendus outre-Rhin, 94 en France). Aujourd'hui, en cette veille de vacances pascales, un septième long métrage produit et réalisé aussi à Berlin, sort sur nos écrans: *Astérix et les Indiens*. Ou les tribulations, contées par Pierre Tchernia, du petit moustachu teigneux, de son compère enrobé et du druide Panoramix, partis sans le vouloir à la découverte du Nouveau Monde. Inspirée de *la Grande Traversée*, cette nouvelle adaptation cinématographique a donné naissance à un livre, réservé comme elle aux plus jeunes fans. Hormis l'esprit qui rend chères à leurs aînés les BD d'Astérix, ils y trouveront toutes les autres constantes des albums, de la crétinerie des Romains à la gloutonnerie d'Obélix, en passant par les poissons avariés d'Ordralphabétix et les inévitables baffes qu'ils provoquent. La saga continue...

**Isabelle PIA**

## Leçons d'humour dans un parc

▪ Situé au cœur de la forêt d'Ermenonville, dans l'Oise, et imprégné de l'esprit de la fameuse bande dessinée, le parc Astérix n'affichait pourtant pas, depuis son ouverture, en 1989, un chiffre d'affaires glorieux. Avec une fréquentation en hausse de 32% l'an dernier (1 554 000 visiteurs), qui lui a permis de réaliser ses quinze premiers millions de bénéfices – alors que Disneyland Paris faiblit –, le parc Astérix va entamer sa septième saison le 8 avril plus sereinement et riche de deux nouvelles attractions. Vous serez donc invité à combattre, dans la Cité grecque, l'Hydre de Lerne à sept têtes et à vous embarquer sur des menhirs flottants qui vous feront découvrir un nouveau quartier, le Domaine lacustre, mais aussi chavirer dans un tunnel et plonger dans le lac par une chute de 13 mètres de haut... Ceux qui ne goûtent pas les sensations fortes pourront toujours se rabattre sur les spectacles de rue, sur la revue de music-hall se déroulant dans les arènes ou sur les iguanes et les tortues géantes des Galapagos qui évoluent sur un écran en trois dimensions.

I.P.

*Infos visiteurs au 36. 68.30.10 et sur minitel 36 15 PARC ASTERIX.*

Astérix et les Indiens, *un film de Gerhard Hahn.*
Astérix et les Indiens,
*éd. Albert René, 52p., 52F.*
(1) Toutastérix *de Marc Jallon, Ifrane Editions.*

(i) Trouvez dans le texte les mots ou les phrases dont les expressions ci-dessous sont les équivalents:

(a) qui décrit ce qui se passe en Amérique

.................................................................................................................... (1)

(b) essayent désespérément de trouver

.................................................................................................................... (1)

(c) qui a connu un grand succès quand il a été publié

.................................................................................................................... (1)

(d) faisant naître beaucoup d'admiration

.................................................................................................................... (1)

(e) incarne

.................................................................................................................... (1)

(f) aux enthousiastes d'Astérix

.................................................................................................................... (1)

(g) qui va probablement inciter

.................................................................................................................... (1)

(h) sur lesquels se trouve le portrait d'Astérix

.................................................................................................................... (1)

(i) cette admiration étonnante

.................................................................................................................... (1)

(j) était sûr d'exciter l'attention de

.................................................................................................................... (1)

(k) pour découvrir l'Amérique

.................................................................................................................... (1)

(l)  ceux qui sont plus âgés qu'eux

......................................................................................................................  (1)

**(ii)** Référez-vous au paragraphe qui s'intitule 'Leçons d'humour dans un parc'. Vous trouverez ci-dessous des chiffres (à gauche) et des définitions (à droite). A vous de décider quelle définition va avec chaque chiffre. Attention! Il y a plus de définitions que de chiffres.

| 1 | 2 | 3 | 4 | 5 | 6 |
|---|---|---|---|---|---|
|   |   |   |   |   |   |

**Chiffres**

**1**  32%

**2**  1 554 000

**3**  6

**4**  1989

**5**  15 000 000

**6**  7

**Définitions**

(a)  année dans laquelle les premiers visiteurs ont pu aller au parc

(b)  périodes d'ouverture déjà complétées

(c)  hauteur de la chute d'eau

(d)  profit (en francs) déjà accumulé

(e)  têtes du monstre légendaire

(f)  personnes qui ont visité le parc l'année dernière

(g)  augmentation du nombre de visiteurs

(6)

## En raison de la grève

# Les SDF privés de métro

*D'habitude, la RATP organise quatre tournées quotidiennes de soutien aux sans-abri.*

Hier, pour cause de trafic nul, les grilles des stations de métro se sont fermées. Au nez des usagers. Au nez des sans domicile fixe aussi. Les quelques centaines de personnes qui se réfugient quotidiennement en ces lieux n'ont pu accéder aux bancs qui leur servent de lits. Et, hier, devant les portes closes, certains Parisiens s'inquiétaient du sort de ces exclus.

### Opération Atlas

*« Il faut voir plus loin que cela et éviter de raisonner de manière émotive,* explique le docteur Patrick Henry, qui occupe une fonction de conseil à la RATP. *A première vue, le métro apparaît à ces personnes en difficulté comme un refuge. Or, il s'avère que ce refuge se transforme vite en piège. Sous terre, un individu perd ses repères spatiaux et temporels. Il vit toujours dans le même bruit, la même odeur, la même température. Il n'a plus la notion du temps et s'enfonce peu à peu dans le brouillard. A la différence des personnes qui vivent dans la rue et qui, elles, voient le soleil se lever, suivent l'activité de la foule et ressentent les différences de température. La désocialisation débute avec la perte de ce rythme. »*

Il est très difficile d'évaluer le nombre des personnes qui « habitent » dans le métro. Entre 200 et 1 500 au plus fort de l'hiver. Des chiffres qu'il faut prendre avec précaution. *« Les SDF qui se réfugient dans le métro ne sont qu'une minorité parmi les exclus,* rappelle un représentant d'association. *Mais ce sont ceux que l'on remarque le plus. »*

*« Dans le temps, on les appelait les clochards,* poursuit le docteur Henry. *Il faut absolument aller à leur rencontre. Ils ne viendront pas par eux-mêmes. S'ils restent sous terre, trois semaines peuvent suffire à les détruire. »* A la perte d'identité et de projet, s'ajoutent l'altération des facultés de jugement et la modification du schéma corporel. *« Nous rencontrons des personnes qui ne savent même plus dans quel état elles se trouvent. Elles souffrent pourtant de pathologies épouvantables. »*

De l'avis général, ce processus de désocialisation, qui apparaît également chez les exclus de la rue, est considérablement accéléré en sous-sol. Pour combattre cette situation, le Recueil social de la RATP organise, d'habitude, quatre tournées quotidiennes pour leur venir en aide. Les personnes qui le désirent sont ensuite conduites au centre d'hébergement de Nanterre.

La RATP reconduira également, cette année, l'opération Atlas. La Régie, en collaboration avec le Samu social de Paris, la SNCF et l'Armée du Salut, va mettre en place, en surface, des structures temporaires d'accueil et de soins pour les exclus (Nation, République, gare du Nord et Châtelet).

De son côté, le SAMU social a ouvert, depuis lundi, un service téléphonique de jour (05.30.63.06). Ignorant la grève, tout comme les nombreuses associations qui poursuivent chaque jour un travail de longue haleine.

**Françoise DARGENT**

Complétez les phrases ci-dessous selon le sens du texte.

(a) Les grilles des stations de métro se sont fermées hier parce qu'il ...................................

.................................................................................................................. (1)

(b) D'habitude les stations de métro servent d'abri à ................................................

qui se couchent sur ........................................................................................... (2)

(c) En considérant le problème, on doit essayer de raisonner de façon ................................,

selon Patrick Henry. (1)

(d) Il y a des ................................... aussi bien que des avantages à vivre de cette façon. (1)

(e) Ceux qui vivent dans la rue connaissent un rythme de vie ....................................... (1)

(f) Le chiffre d'habitants du métro n'est pas ............................................................ (1)

(g) Autrefois les SDF étaient dénommés ................................................................ (1)

(h) Les SDF ne veulent pas venir demander de l'aide, alors il est important d'aller les

.................................................................................................................. (1)

(i) Au bout de ............................................... ils risquent de ...........................................

.................................................................................................................. (2)

(j) On croit que ceux qui vivent dans la rue connaissent .............. vite la désocialisation. (1)

(k) Le Recueil social de la RATP fait des tournées quatre fois ....................................... pour
venir à l'aide des SDF du métro. (1)

(l) ........................................... organisations vont mettre en place des structures temporaires
d'accueil pour les SDF. (1)

### Devant la cour d'assises de Seine-Saint-Denis

# L'innocence reconnue de Michel Peuron

*Condamné en 1992 à la réclusion criminelle à perpétuité pour assassinat, il devrait être aujourd'hui réhabilité.*

Sauf coup de théâtre, Michel Peuron sera acquitté ce soir au terme d'une histoire kafkaïenne qui a commencé avec la découverte de sa carte d'assuré social près du corps d'un sans-domicile-fixe à Aubervilliers. En 1992, il a été condamné, par contumace, à la peine maximale : la réclusion criminelle à perpétuité pour assassinat. Le procès d'aujourd'hui doit permettre à Michel Peuron de « purger la contumace » car il a été établi que ce marginal de 42 ans ne pouvait avoir commis le crime pour lequel il avait été emprisonné.

En 1991, un couple de clochards alcooliques, Arsène Paris et Nadia Thibout d'Anesy, occupent un squat d'Aubervilliers (Seine-Saint-Denis). Ils vivent avec un SDF, Christian Tessier, et un autre homme à l'accent basque qu'ils connaissent sous le nom de Michel Peuron. Le 19 février, Tessier annonce à ses compagnons qu'il vient de recevoir une pension de 4 000 francs en liquide. Au cours d'une soirée arrosée, Tessier est roué de coups par les trois comparses. Michel Peuron aurait fait main basse sur l'argent et se serait enfui au matin.

### Le « troisième homme »

Lorsqu'ils comparaissent devant la cour d'assises de Seine-Saint-Denis pour répondre d'assassinat, en mars 1992, Thibout d'Anesy et Paris rejettent une partie de la responsabilité du drame sur un Peuron introuvable. Le jury les reconnaît coupables d'assassinat et de vol. Il les condamne respectivement à 10 et 12 ans d'emprisonnement. Quant à Peuron, dont la carte d'assuré social a été retrouvée dans le squat, il écope de la peine maximale : la réclusion criminelle à perpétuité.

En août 1993, Michel Peuron tombe des nues lorsque les gendarmes l'interpellent. Lui qui n'a pas une pointe d'accent basque dans la voix ignore tout de son statut de « fugitif ». « *Je ne connaissais ni le lieu du crime, ni les complices dont ils parlaient, ni la victime* », se souvient-il. Il a beau clamer son innocence, il est incarcéré.

Michel Peuron observe une grève de la faim et de la soif de dix jours. Il est finalement entendu par un juge d'instruction au début de l'année 1994. Pour la première fois, il est confronté au couple condamné pour assassinat. Paris et Thibout d'Anesy sont formels : ils ne l'ont jamais vu. Le magistrat décide donc de sa remise en liberté sous contrôle judiciaire. Entre temps, Michel Peuron a passé cinq mois en détention préventive.

Un supplément d'information permet d'établir que Peuron se trouvait à Nantes au moment des faits. C'est lui qui fournit la clef de l'énigme aux enquêteurs. Le « troisième homme » serait l'une de ses connaissances, un sans-domicile-fixe qu'il a hébergé à Nantes. En 1990, il lui aurait dérobé ses papiers d'identité avant de s'enfuir. Un mandat d'arrêt est lancé contre le meurtrier présumé qui est bientôt interpellé. Me Yvon Chotard, l'avocat de Michel Peuron, profitera du procès pour dénoncer les lacunes de la procédure. Pour une fois, réquisitoire et plaidoirie se ressembleront étrangement.

**Éric PELLETIER (*avec AFP*)**

Faites le récit des événements en mettant les phrases ci-dessous dans le bon ordre.

| Examiner's tip | You will probably change your mind about the order as you do the exercise. Write your answers in the boxes in pencil first of all, so that you can change them easily; remember to write them in ink when you have made your final decision, as most Boards insist on this. |

**Examiner's tip** You will probably change your mind about the order as you do the exercise. Write your answers in the boxes in pencil first of all, so that you can change them easily; remember to write them in ink when you have made your final decision, as most Boards insist on this.

If you change your mind later, cross out the letter you no longer want, and write your new answer clearly at the side or underneath. **Never** try to change one letter into another.

| 1 | 2 | 3 | 4 | 5 | 6 | 7 | 8 | 9 | 10 |
|---|---|---|---|---|---|---|---|---|----|
|   |   |   |   |   |   |   |   |   |    |

(a) La police a interrogé Peuron.

(b) Tessier a été assassiné.

(c) Les trois SDF ont été condamnés.

(d) On a trouvé un document qui appartenait à Peuron.

(e) On a découvert que Peuron n'était pas impliqué dans le crime.

(f) Un SDF a volé les papiers d'identité de Peuron.

(g) Tessier a reçu une grande somme d'argent.

(h) Peuron a refusé la nourriture.

(i) Peuron a comparu devant le juge d'instruction.

(j) Les deux inculpés ont accusé Peuron d'avoir participé au crime.

(10)

# Why the French adore l'Oxford St

## The Chunnel and a strong franc have brought new élan to the West End, finds **Ross Clark**

FEBRUARY in London might not quite have the same romantic connotations as April in Paris, but that is a small matter for the hoards which, in increasing numbers, are flooding off the morning Eurostars at Waterloo. *Les Day-Trippers* have arrived. According to Eurostar, the French are coming over at the rate of 5,000 each weekday. That is over 10 jumbo-jet loads, although no airline ever did remotely as much to promote Anglo-French trade. And it is still only February, two months before the start of the tourist season.

At an exchange rate of seven-and-a-half francs to the pound, it is perhaps not hard to see why so many French are flocking to London. A recent survey revealed that booze is now just about the only thing which is cheaper in France than England. While our own countryfolk can afford no grander day out than the drunken "bottle run" to a Calais hypermarket, Parisians and the good people of Lille – are they correctly known as Lilliputians? – are coming for grand days out dedicated to *le shopping* in Oxford Street. They are stocking up in perfume at up D. H. Evans, scooping up whole sides of smoked salmon in Harrods Food Hall. They are even buying our suits.

I caught two Lilliputians sifting their way through the bargain rails in a narrow Oxford Street store called Suit's You. The shop seemed to have known they were coming, for there were few of the usual creased, double-breasted, slightly pin-striped suits which have become standard issue for our own business types; just rack upon rack of the fine-grained, greenish-brown Eurotweed which European yuppies always seem to wear in adverts for male scent.

"What made you come all the way to London to buy suits?" I asked them.

"Why do we come? I think you English may be right about not liking the European currency, after all. Le franc goes a very long way, I think. Thank you."

There is something absurdly relaxed about French businessmen: it as if they had been trained to spend their entire lives snooping about the shops in white raincoats. Whether the jewellery was for Madame or her rival, one did not like to ask.

For if there is one class of people excluded from the latest French invasion, it is wives. True, I did find one lady fawning over the glazed pâtés in Selfridges' Food Hall – which I thought was just too much like sending the coals to Newcastle. But then she turned out to live in Kensington.

They are not just here to shop, the French. You may have noticed they are filling up our museums and art galleries, too, photographing one another on the stairs, shuffling through posters

**Chic by jowl** A pair of well-dressed consumers, fresh off the Eurostar

in the shops and even looking at one or two paintings.

To Cambridge Circus, and the queue to see *Les Misérables*. There were three copies of *Le Monde* being read, the odd whiff of Gauloise and still more Eurotweed suits.

"Why come all the way to London to see a show about Parisian urchins?" I asked a group of girls.

"So many shows. And so funny. Nobody does it like a steam train."

They seemed to find this particularly amusing. Though I didn't like to tell them that if *Starlight Express* – the show whose slogan they repeated – was what they wanted they were in the wrong queue.

They all end, *Les Day-Trippers*, back at Waterloo Station at 27 minutes past six, when the last Eurostar rolls away from the platform. Before the departure, the bar, placed so strategically opposite the departure gates, is a picture of jollity which Waterloo can rarely have seen before. Those Jacques Attalis in white raincoats sink their brandies so much more sociably than the few ruddy-faced Surrey commuters who have taken to drink rather than face the early train home.

There, disappearing through the departure gates, was the very same Lilliputian whom I saw in the suit shop, now burdened with plastic bags.

"You are very hospitable people, I think. And so much quicker to get to than Paris. Perhaps I should come here to work every day, though I don't think I want to earn your pounds."

And with the smile of a lottery winner he strode off towards the escalator, a pair of new shoes tapping on the tiled floor: the picture of a suave Frenchman, perhaps, had it not been let down a little bit by the Dolcis bag.

Répondez en français aux questions ci-dessous.

**1**  Quel moyen de transport les Français utilisent-ils pour venir à Londres, selon l'article?

......................................................................................................................... (1)

**2**  Pourquoi est-ce que tant de Français viennent faire du shopping à Londres?

.........................................................................................................................

......................................................................................................................... (2)

**3**  Qu'est-ce qu'ils achètent?

.........................................................................................................................

......................................................................................................................... (3)

**4**  A part les magasins, où vont-ils?

.........................................................................................................................

......................................................................................................................... (2)

**5**  Quel contraste l'auteur de l'article a-t-il remarqué entre les Français et les Anglais?

.........................................................................................................................

......................................................................................................................... (2)

**6**  Pourquoi le Lillois ne voudrait-il pas travailler à Londres?

.........................................................................................................................

......................................................................................................................... (1)

You could also use this article as the basis for an interpretation exercise for the oral test.

**TASK K** Traduisez l'article ci-dessous en anglais.

---

### LE MOT DE LA SEMAINE

**// Le Canada n'est pas un véritable pays. Il compte deux peuples, deux nations et deux territoires. //**

Lucien Bouchard,
Premier ministre du Québec

Le nouveau Premier ministre du Québec reste fidèle aux idéaux et à la faconde qui l'ont rendu si populaire auprès de ses concitoyens. Lundi, Lucien Bouchard a comme prévu succédé à Jacques Parizeau, le chef du gouvernement démissionnaire qui avait précédemment annoncé son retrait de la vie politique.

Bouchard avait été le principal animateur de la campagne en faveur du oui au référendum sur la souveraineté du Québec, perdu de peu par les « souverainistes » le 30 octobre dernier. En présentant son gouvernement, il a annoncé que son principal objectif serait l'assainissement des finances publiques, afin que le Québec accède un jour à l'indépendance « *sur des bases financières et sociales solides* ».

(25)

# MEDECINE

## Les familles et leur médecin

# Un comportement de consommateurs

*Les Français sont en majorité fidèles à leur médecin, mais sont devenus exigeants.*
*Faut-il remplacer le paiement à l'acte par un abonnement?*

Quelle est la place du généraliste « dans un système de santé en quête d'économies » ? Pour répondre à cette question, la Fédération des familles de France a enquêté parmi les 160 000 familles qu'elle réunit. Pour Jacques Bichot, son président, les résultats de ce travail *« révèlent chez un grand nombre de personnes interrogées un comportement de consommateur et non de patient ».*

Pratiquement deux mille réponses sont parvenues aux enquêteurs. L'échantillonnage n'est, certes pas représentatif de la population française, les femmes et les personnes plus de 50 ans étant majoritaires. Ces réponses font néanmoins apparaître d'intéressantes tendances.

Dans la population interrogée, la majorité des personnes consultent le même médecin généraliste depuis 10 à 20 ans. Près de 60% d'entre elles trouvent normal que les divers membres d'une même famille consultent habituellement des généralistes différents.

Toutefois, au problème de la trangression du secret médical en cas de sida, les trois quarts des personnes ayant répondu à cette question pensent que le médecin « peut » informer la famille d'un enfant mineur. Dans l'ensemble, elles sont encore 53,3 % a estimer que les médecins peuvent transgresser ce secret lorsqu'il s'agit d'un majeur. *« La question du secret médical mérite largement d'être, non seulement approfondie, mais doit surtout faire l'objet d'un véritable travail d'explication auprès des familles (...) quelle que soit la maladie rencontrée »,* soulignent les représentants de la Fédération.

Les personnes interrogées demandent au généraliste de se déplacer à domicile (86 %) à toute heure du jour, et de la nuit pour trois quarts d'entre elles, et le week-end (70 %). Les plus âgés manifestent le moins l'exigence d'une disponibilité permanente du généraliste.

Parallèlement, nombreux sont ceux (63 %) qui consultent directement un spécialiste. En tête, le gynécologue, puis le pédiatre enfin, le cardiologue, beaucoup plus souvent consulté directement par les hommes de la quarantaine. Une minorité notable (28,1 %) consulte plusieurs spécialistes pour la même affection. 7,3 % déclarent agir ainsi de manière habituelle.

Nombre de personnes (45,3 %) ne sont pas hostiles aux certificats de complaisance. En premier, vient l'ajout, sur l'ordonnance de médicaments achetés de son propre chef et qui, autrement, ne seraient pas remboursés par l'Assurance Maladie. On trouve, en seconde position les certificats de dispense d'activité sportive. Puis, viennent les demandes d'arrêt de travail. Les plus âgés, eux, sont sensibles au fait de pouvoir obtenir une attestation permettant de demander une procuration électorale.

### Rapport qualité/prix

La compétence est la qualité la plus importante demandée au généraliste. Il est, analysent les auteurs de l'enquête, *« perçu comme un technicien ».* Pour 70 % la formation du généraliste est satisfaisante. Mais, les principaux reproches formulés sont le manque de formation continue et le manque de psychologie. Et, plus de la moitié des personnes interrogées remarquent que leur médecin généraliste... ne se lave pas les mains avant de commencer à les examiner.

Dans le contexte actuel, la Fédération note: *« Il ne s'agit pàs d'instaurer un rationnement des soins mais d'améliorer leur rapport qualité/prix. Le médecin généraliste peut-il jouer un rôle dans cette croissance de l'efficacité ? »*

Reprenant à son compte les propositions tendant à faire du généraliste le *« médecin de référence centralisant et synthétisant les données médicales concernant un patient »,* la Fédération des familles de France va plus loin que les projets actuels et propose de *« réfléchir à une sorte d'abonnement remplaçant le paiement à l'acte »,* afin d'éviter au médecin la tentation de les multiplier.

*« S'il était, de plus, chargé de gérer le budget santé de ses patients, réfléchit la Fédération, il ne prescrirait que des médicaments utiles, sélectionnerait les hôpitaux, les laboratoires ou les kinésithérapeutes ayant un bon rapport qualité/prix. »*

**Mireille DIDIER**

(i) Exprimez **en vos propres termes** le sens des locutions suivantes, qui se trouvent dans les 2e et 3e paragraphes du texte.

(a) pratiquement deux mille réponses sont parvenues aux enquêteurs

..................................................................................................................................

.......................................................................................................................... (3)

(b) les femmes et les personnes plus de 50 ans étant majoritaires

..................................................................................................................................

.......................................................................................................................... (3)

(c) font néanmoins apparaître d'intéressantes tendances

..................................................................................................................................

.......................................................................................................................... (4)

(d) dans la population interrogée

..................................................................................................................................

.......................................................................................................................... (2)

(e) consultent le même médecin généraliste depuis 10 à 20 ans

..................................................................................................................................

.......................................................................................................................... (3)

(ii) Answer the following questions in English.

(a) What did the survey discover with regard to people's attitudes about AIDS?

..................................................................................................................................

.......................................................................................................................... (2)

(b) What do the figures 86% and 70% represent?

.......................................................................................................................... (2)

(c) Which three specialists head the list of doctors consulted?

.......................................................................................................................... (3)

(d) In what way can older people benefit from a doctor's certificate?

.......................................................................................................... (1)

(e) What did the people questioned in the survey see as the most important factor in their choice of a GP?

.......................................................................................................... (1)

(f) What comment was made by more than half of those questioned?

..........................................................................................................

.......................................................................................................... (2)

(g) How does the *Fédération* sum up the current situation?

..........................................................................................................

.......................................................................................................... (3)

(h) What are its proposals, and why?

..........................................................................................................

..........................................................................................................

.......................................................................................................... (4)

DOSSIER

# ÉTUDIANTS : VIVRE ENSEMBLE

**Suivre les mêmes cours ne suffit pas toujours à créer des liens entre les étudiants. La vie en dehors de l'université est tout aussi capitale. D'où l'importance des associations.**

Qui dit université dit aussi «zinzin» et autres soirées dansantes, sport ou cinéma. Les étudiants doivent ainsi concilier pendant quelques années travail et distraction. Dans notre département, comment se passe l'existence quotidienne de tous ceux qui fréquentent les universités, de création toute récente, ou l'I.U.T. de Béthune, bien plus ancien (l'établissement va en effet fêter prochainement son quart de siècle) ?

Les résultats obtenus par nos étudiants lors des rencontres sportives nationales, ou encore le succès remporté en mai dernier par les fêtes du sport (rassemblant des étudiants de l'ensemble des pôles de l'université d'Artois), démontrent que les clubs et associations du département jouent parfaitement leur rôle.

### A titre d'exemple

«Pour qu'une association, *sportive ou autre, fonctionne bien, il faut qu'elle ait déjà un à deux ans d'existence*», explique la présidente de *Déclic*, qui regroupe en son sein les étudiants de l'école universitaire de science économique et de gestion (EUSEG), installée à Béhune. *Déclic* est l'une des associations d'étudiants les plus actives du département. Cette année, elle a mis sur pied une «semaine d'intégration» réservée aux nouveaux élèves de l'établissement. Rien à voir avec le traditionnel bizutage; simplement, durant deux sessions de trois jours, étudiants (anciens et nouveaux) et professeurs se retrouvent hors de l'enceinte sco-

laire pour mieux se connaître et mettre au point le programme de l'année. L'expérience sera d'ailleurs reconduite à la rentrée prochaine.

Les étudiants béthunois ne sont pas les seuls à créer des associations. Il en existe une par filière universitaire. A Boulogne et surtout à Calais (où certaines filières ont presque vingt ans d'âge), les associations d'étudiants commencent à prendre de l'ampleur. A Boulogne, une maison de l'étudiant sera même créée, et gérée par une association composée de représentants institutionnels (université, district urbain) et d'étudiants. Mais pour l'instant, ce sont souvent les associations à vocation sportive qui attirent du monde. A Boulogne notamment vient de s'achever, avec un succès réel, la première régate des grandes écoles de la région.

But avoué de ces multiples associations: créer l'ambiance, faire naître une réelle solidarité et combattre le plus possible l'individualisme. «*Il faut éviter que chacun aille en cours sans se préoccuper des autres*, explique cet étudiant de deuxième année d'anglais qui ajoute: *beaucoup rentrent chez eux le soir, ce qui ne facilite pas les rencontres*».

Effectivement, une étude menée par le district d'Arras démontre que c'est seulement à partir de la licence que les étudiants quittent le logement familial et optent pour la chambre en ville. Les autres préfèrent rester chez leurs parents, et passent de ce fait beaucoup de temps dans les transports.

Difficile dans ce cas de prendre part à la vie de la faculté, du quartier ou de la cité.

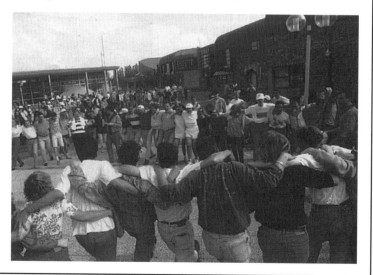

**(i)** Lisez le texte, puis décidez si les constatations ci-dessous sont vraies (V) ou fausses (F).

V    F

**1**   Ceux qui étudient les mêmes matières à l'université se retrouvent toujours pendant leurs heures de loisirs. ☐ ☐

**2**   On a réuni les étudiants de toutes les facultés pour des concours sportifs. ☐ ☐

**3**   Déclic rassemble étudiants et professeurs pour une période de cinq jours. ☐ ☐

**4**   On vient de créer une maison de l'étudiant à Boulogne. ☐ ☐

**5**   L'objectif des associations est d'éveiller l'esprit de fraternité chez les étudiants. ☐ ☐ (5)

**(ii)** Trouvez dans le texte les mots qui correspondent aux définitions ou aux synonymes ci-dessous:

**1**   trouver un équilibre entre ............................................................... (1)

**2**   bientôt ............................................................... (1)

**3**   circonscription administrative locale ............................................. (1)

**4**   ce qui entoure ............................................................... (1)

**5**   renouvelée ............................................................... (1)

**6**   être mené à bien ............................................................... (1)

**7**   tendance à s'affirmer indépendemment des autres .............................. (1)

**(iii)** Answer the following questions in English:

**1**   What question is being asked at the beginning of the article?

............................................................... (1)

**2**   What is *Déclic*, and what comment does its president make?

...............................................................

............................................................... (3)

**3**   What does the survey carried out by the district of Arras show?

...............................................................

...............................................................

............................................................... (5)

## Pour remonter le temps, choisissez votre route !

Pour[1] de château en château, la Haute-Garonne vous offre le choix des itinéraires et la possibilité d'[2] une multitude de circuits à thème. La Route du Pastel est bien évidemment celle qui vous[3] de découvrir le plus grand nombre de sites historiques, en vous[4] de Toulouse à St-Géry, par St-Félix de Lauragais, Sorèze, Puylaurens, Magrin et, plus au nord, Lavaur.

Pour remonter davantage les siècles,[5] la Route Préhistorique Romaine. Celle-ci vous[6] au cœur du Comminges, ancienne province de la Gascogne, entre Aurignac, Saint-Bertrand et Montmaurin. Grottes préhistoriques, villes et villas galloromaines… En chemin, la Haute-Garonne vous[7] une histoire passionnante. Ou,[8] votre bâton et progressez sur les pas de Saint-Jacques-de-Compostelle. Ce périple de Toulouse à Saint-Bertrand-de-Comminges vous propose pour étapes, une multitude d'églises, cathédrales, monastères.

*En Haute-Garonne,*
*tous les marchés sont hauts en couleurs.*

*Sport, nature et eaux sauvages.*

## Entre deux châteaux, prenez le temps de savourer les délices de la vie en Haute-Garonne.

Amoureux de nature, vous préférerez probablement suivre la Garonne en traversant le département de nord en sud. Ou suivre la Route des Grands Espaces, de Saint-Gaudens à Bourg d'Oueil près de Bagnères-de-Luchon. De paysages vallonnés en montagnes grandioses, ouvrez grands les yeux et respirez à fond : crêtes vertigineuses, cascades bondissantes, troupeaux de moutons guidés par un vieux berger, villages isolés… C'est un autre monde que vous découvrirez, à pied, à cheval, en VTT, en canoë… Ou pourquoi pas d'un peu plus haut, en parapente ou en deltaplane, très pratiqués dans la région de Luchon.

La route des Vins vous invite quant à elle à découvrir une autre Haute-Garonne. Celle des autres château (viticoles ceux là !) et des plaisirs de la table. Avec arrêt obligatoire à Fronton, fief de l'appellation des Côtes du Frontonnais, devenue Appellation d'Origine Contrôlée depuis 1975. Mais aussi à Vacquiers, a Saint-Rustice, à Bessières où de nombreux propriétaires pratiquent la vente directe… Sans oublier Castelnau d'Estrétefond, haut-lieu du foie gras, du confit et de l'incontournable cassoulet.

*Découvrez la Haute-Garonne en VTT.*

*Plaisir de la table*
*avec un gratin de poires aux truffes.*

**(i)** Vous trouverez ci-dessous une liste de verbes. A vous de choisir ceux dont vous avez besoin pour remplir les blancs dans la première partie du texte. Attention! Il y a plus de verbes que de blancs.

| | | | |
|---|---|---|---|
| aller | emprunter | permettrez | suivez |
| conduira | laissez | prenez | |
| conduisant | permettra | racontera | |

**1** .............................................

**2** .............................................

**3** .............................................

**4** .............................................

**5** .............................................

**6** .............................................

**7** .............................................

**8** ............................................. (8)

**(ii)** Traduisez en anglais le quatrième paragraphe du texte ('Amoureux de nature' – 'dans la région de Luchon')

.............................................................................................................

.............................................................................................................

.............................................................................................................

.............................................................................................................

.............................................................................................................

.............................................................................................................

.............................................................................................................

............................................................................................................. (20)

**(iii)** Remplissez les blancs dans les phrases ci-dessous selon le sens du cinquième paragraphe ('La Route des vins' – 'cassoulet')

En prenant la Route des vins vous ............................................ une autre Haute-Garonne. Là, dans les châteaux on cultive des ..................................... Il ......................... absolument s'arrêter à Fronton; visitez aussi Vacquiers, Saint-Rustice et Bessières où plusieurs propriétaires ........................................ leur vin directement au grand public.

A Castelnau d'Estrétefond on peut goûter des ........................................ gastronomiques.

(5)

*Letts* **Q&A**

TASK O

## Le point de...

### Jean-François Revel
# Coupables silences

**A vouloir trop longtemps ignorer la violence à l'école, on a fini par la laisser tout envahir. La dissimulation de cette tragédie est un crime contre la démocratie.**

**P**lusieurs bubons d'insécurité dans les écoles viennent brusquement d'éclater. En France, quand ces éruptions au grand jour se produisent, c'est que des foyers d'infection étaient cachés depuis longtemps. La tendance française est de voiler tant qu'on le peut la gravité des abus. Regardez l'ARC: toutes les révélations du rapport de la Cour des comptes étaient connues des gouvernements successifs depuis des années grâce à un rapport de l'Inspection générale des affaires sociales, qui avait été étouffé.

Il en est allé de même pour ce qu'il faut bien appeler la criminalité et la délinquance dans les lycées et collèges. Ce n'est pas d'aujourd'hui qu'elles sévissent, mais l'administration détestait en parler. Des proviseurs tremblants assuraient que ce n'était pas la peine d'en faire un drame. Ils dissuadaient les parents des victimes de porter plainte. Lorsque les lycéens eux-mêmes ont manifesté, en 1990, pour réclamer davantage de surveillants, une certaine bonne presse les a traités de réactionnaires, voire de racistes.

La violence à l'école ne s'explique pas seulement par la misère des « quartiers ». Pas plus qu'en Corse les diagnostics purement économiques ne suffisent. La délinquance provient aussi de ce qu'il est beaucoup moins pénible de voler, de violer, d'extorquer, de trafiquer des drogues que de faire des études. Et les jeunes n'ont aucune raison de se gêner, à partir du moment où ils constatent que ces fructueux débordements ne rencontrent aucune résistance de la part des autorités.

L'indispensable traitement des causes sociales de cette dégradation ne dispense nullement de commencer par en combattre les conséquences criminelles. Or, actuellement, nous en sommes au stade des faux-fuyants vertueux. On a même vu un professeur de collège déclarer à la télévision, le 26 janvier, qu'il était très heureux d'avoir reçu un coup de poing d'un élève, ou soi-disant tel, parce que cela nouait le dialogue. Il y a des masochistes partout, mais le masochisme n'a jamais servi à garantir le droit.

Un autre remède proposé a été de projeter aux cogneurs et dévaliseurs un film de quinze minutes les incitant à se radoucir. Merveille! Quarante-cinq minutes feront l'affaire, j'imagine, pour transformer en agneaux les coupables d'agressions à main armée. Saisissons sans tarder la Commission d'avance sur recettes. Ces sornettes sauveront à coup sûr le cinéma français.

On voit bien ce qui inspire ce feu d'artifice de bonnes intentions stériles : le principe que la prévention est préférable à la répression. Comme c'est vrai! Mais la prévention, c'était il y a quinze ans qu'il fallait y penser. On prévient une maladie avant qu'elle ne se déclare, pas quand elle atteint le stade final où le patient doit de toute urgence passer sur le billard. Prévenir consiste à empêcher le fléau de naître. Lorsqu'on a pris soin de le laisser tout envahir, il faut bien le juguler. La dissimulation de cette tragédie a été un crime contre la démocratie. Car comment les jeunes Français se prépareraient-ils à une vie publique républicaine si le modèle de société qu'ils vivent à l'école s'apparente à la jungle primitive ?

François Bayrou (France 3, le 27 janvier) s'est félicité d'un reportage montrant des élèves décidés à prendre eux-mêmes en main leur sécurité. Puis-je, en toute estime et amitié, faire observer au ministre de l'Education nationale que l'Etat républicain n'a pas à se décharger sur des particuliers, surtout mineurs, du devoir de faire régner la sécurité ? Bien plus: c'est illégal. Nul citoyen n'a le droit de se faire justice lui-même ni de se substituer à la police. Encourager de telles initiatives, n'est-ce pas implicitement reconnaître que les écoles aussi sont en train de devenir des zones de non-droit ?

■

Most Exam Boards do not now require formal translation from English into French, preferring to test your understanding by setting questions and exercises of the non-verbal type (such as you have already been practising in this unit) or by asking you to summarise the main points of an article.

**(i)** If your Board sets passages for translation into French, try the following, which is based on the first two paragraphs of the article. If you do not have to do this kind of exercise, use the English passage to help you to understand the rest of the text.

Successive governments in France have tended to cover up as far as possible the fact that serious problems of law and order exist. This has certainly been the case with delinquency and indeed crime in schools; no-one has liked to talk about it. Headmasters, afraid of the possible consequences, have stated that there is no point in making a fuss about the matter. Victims' parents have been persuaded not to complain. In 1990 some newspapers even said that the pupils who were demonstrating in the streets, asking for more supervisors in schools, were motivated by racism. (25)

**(ii)** The second part of the task refers to the next two paragraphs of the text ('*La violence*' – '*garantir le droit*')

Répondez en français aux questions ci-dessous. Il n'est pas nécessaire d'écrire des phrases complètes.

(a) Selon le texte, quelles sont les raisons de la délinquance?

........................................................................................................................

........................................................................................................... (3)

(b) Quelle semble être la réaction des autorités?

........................................................................................................................

........................................................................................................... (1)

(c) Qu'est-ce qu'il faut faire pour mettre fin à la violence?

........................................................................................................................

........................................................................................................... (2)

(d) Qu'est-ce qui a surpris l'auteur de l'article?

........................................................................................................... (2)

**(iii)** The third part of the task refers to the last three paragraphs of the text (*'L'autre remède'* – *'non-droit'*).

Décidez laquelle des réponses possibles termine correctement chaque phrase ci-dessous. Cochez (✓) la bonne réponse.

**1** En entendant la nouvelle du film qu'on a proposé, l'auteur de l'article a été

    (a) ravi          ..........

    (b) incrédule     ..........

    (c) coupable     ..........

**2** Quant à la prévention de la délinquance, l'auteur croit

    (a) qu'il est temps d'y penser     ..........

    (b) qu'on doit y penser dans quinze ans     ..........

    (c) qu'on aurait dû y penser plus tôt     ..........

**3** Selon lui, la solution serait

    (a) de dissimuler     ..........

    (b) d'envahir     ..........

    (c) de l'arrêter avec force     ..........

**4** La société actuelle lui semble

    (a) sauvage     ..........

    (b) préhistorique     ..........

    (c) républicaine     ..........

**5** Selon l'auteur, la possibilité que les élèves s'occupent de leur propre sécurité serait

    (a) bonne     ..........

    (b) mauvaise     ..........

    (c) juste     ..........

(5)

## ASSESSMENT OBJECTIVES

The accuracy of your written French will be taken into account to some extent in the comprehension papers (at least, in the questions which require verbal answers). It is usually less important in the Listening than in the Reading element, provided of course that what you write can be understood. In the essay paper or papers the quality of what you write becomes very important. If your topic essay is written in English, which is still an option with one or two Boards, it is the content that matters most, although the ways in which you express yourself and structure your essays are also taken into consideration. If your essays have to be written in French, the type of language you use and your grammatical accuracy are usually equally important (this may not be the case if you are given the choice of whether to write in French or English). You will find comments on particular points of grammar following the sample essays below. There are several ways in which you can improve the standard of your writing. Some of them apply to any type of essay, and others only to essays on a topic that has been studied in detail.

## EXAMINATION TECHNIQUE

### General points

❶ Check how many words you are allowed to use, and keep within these limits. If you are given a wide range, e.g. 250–400, it makes sense to aim towards the higher number, unless you have a really succinct style. Do not go over the word limit – at least, not by more than a sentence or so – because examiners are sometimes instructed not to mark anything beyond the upper limit. This means that you might lose marks for the structure of your essay (your conclusion might not be taken into account, for example). You may think that the examiner will not know how many words you have used, particularly if your handwriting is small, but don't count on it. Examiners who mark hundreds of essays every year soon develop a 'feel' for the correct length.

How should you go about counting your words? Exam Boards vary in their advice they give on this, but as a general rule they consider a 'word' to be an item of French that has a space on each side of it. Don't spend too much time counting, or worry that you may have miscalculated the final total; as long as you think, after a quick count, that you are within the limits, you are unlikely to be too far outside in either direction.

❷ Read the essay titles carefully. You are almost certain to be given a choice, in either the general essay or the topic paper or both (if your Board sets both; not all of them do so). Consider all the implications of the question. If you are not sure whether you fully understand it, don't try to answer it! Marks are always awarded for relevance to the title; by the same token, marks are lost for irrelevance. You must not churn out an essay that you have prepared in class, unless of course you happen to be presented with **exactly** the same title (see below for how to interpret essay titles). Take your time to decide which essay or essays you will write. It's time well spent, however eager you are to get started.

❸ Plan your essay carefully. Marks are allocated for structure; this means that there should be an introduction and a conclusion, and that the main body of the essay should be well balanced (i.e. if you are considering two different sides to a question, you should aim at writing about the same amount for each).

Do not underestimate the importance of the introduction and conclusion. Your first paragraph is your opportunity to arouse the interest of the examiner; you need him or her to think right from the beginning 'This candidate knows something about the subject'. The conclusion is your final chance to impress; at this point the examiner should be thinking 'This candidate has pulled together all the threads from the main body of the essay and made it into a coherent whole'. As for the main body of your essay, if you have written the introduction carefully you should be able to refer to it in each of your subsequent paragraphs.

In the sample essays below you will find two essay plans which will give you an idea of how you might approach two particular questions. When you are revising, it is an excellent idea to write plans for a number of possible titles related to the topic you have chosen; it is just as useful as writing the whole essays, perhaps even more so if you are working on your own and are unlikely to be able to have a full essay corrected.

**4** Keep an eye on the time while you are writing your essay in the examination itself. Let us suppose that you have taken five minutes to decide which question you will choose, and 10–15 minutes (at least) to write your plan. If your essay is to be written in French, you must allow yourself time to check your accuracy when you have finished it. It's very easy, in the stress of the moment, to leave off adjective agreements or put the wrong ending on a verb. These are expensive errors and you cannot afford to make them. This applies even more if you are trying to write a fair copy of your answer in the last minutes of the time allowed (not usually to be recommended anyway); there is no point in working out carefully what you want to say and how to say it, if you throw it all away by rushing it at the end. You cannot change your character; if you know you work quickly and carelessly you must train yourself to check what you have written. If you work slowly and more thoroughly in the first place, less checking time (but some, nevertheless) is necessary at the end.

**5** Many coursebooks and some dictionaries include a list of phrases that may be used to improve your writing style. These are often 'linking' phrases which come at the beginning of a paragraph; e.g. *il faut peser le pour et le contre, en revanche, il faut également noter que …, commençons par le côté positif* etc. Used properly and in moderation these are good, but don't sprinkle them wildly through your essay regardless of their precise meaning, and don't use too many of them. The examiner wants to see what you know about the subject you have chosen, and is not interested in reading a succession of pre-learned phrases alternating with brief comments. Besides, they all use up your allocation of words which would be better spent in expressing your opinions and in illustrating the points you are making.

## Specific points relating to topic essays

**1** Make a list of precise topic-related vocabulary, under the three headings of nouns, verbs and adjectives, and learn it. For literature, this means knowing words such as *personnage* and *caractère* (and the difference between them), *l'écrivain*, *l'auteur*, specific words relating to plays and/or novels, adjectives to describe the author's style, verbs to explain what the author (and the characters) are doing. For non-literary topics, a different type of list is needed; the range of vocabulary will vary according to the particular subject you are studying. As you read newspaper articles on your chosen theme, note down some useful words. For '*La Violence*' you could look up the words for hooligans, attack, disorder, riots, terrorism, as well as verbs and adjectives linked to them. For '*Les Medias*', look for words to do with advertising (press and television), influence, sway, affect, bias, broadcast, programme etc. Impressionism obviously has its own range of specialist vocabulary linked with painting, techniques, light, subject, and colour. It all sounds very obvious, but it is surprising how few candidates use a wide range of appropriate vocabulary.

**2** Illustrate the points you are making with close reference to the text (literature) or to particular instances (non-literary topics). General comments are all very well, but the examiner will want to know how you have reached this point of view.

**3** Quote. For literature, this means quoting directly from from the text; for non-literary topics, it means using statistics or dates or names of people or places wherever possible. You must be accurate. If your Board allows you to take your text in to the examination you have no excuse for not quoting correctly; even so, you would be well advised to learn a handful of carefully chosen short quotations beforehand, so that you don't waste time looking for them. Find out whether they have to be included in the word count; but anyway, keep them brief, as it is your essay the examiner wants to read and a long quotation can distract the attention from the point being made. Don't overdo it; as a general rule, about four direct quotations an essay is likely to be acceptable, as long as you also illustrate your answer with examples showing, for example, how the character behaves or what happened during a violent confrontation in the streets.

It is easier to remember words than figures, so it is probably better to learn an approximate number (e.g. *à peu près 2,75 millions*) rather than risk getting it completely wrong. It should not be too difficult to remember dates; the year is usually sufficient, though *en septembre 1995* is quite impressive.

**4** Express your own opinions. An essay which merely relates what happens, even if it is correctly slanted to take account of the exact title, will not score as highly as one which also gives a personal viewpoint. Phrases such as *à mon avis* or *je pense que* (these are two separate phrases and should never be used together) and *ce qui me frappe le plus, c'est …* can introduce an element of individualism into your essay.

**5** Spell names correctly! (This applies particularly to essays on literature). Chief examiners complain every year that candidates have been unable to spell the names of the main characters in the novel or play they have been studying, and even spell the name of the author incorrectly. *Anouilh* and *Sartre* cause particular problems. There really is no excuse for this, and it creates a very poor impression.

## How to interpret essay titles (for the Topic paper)

You can be sure that your essay subject will **not** be 'Write all you know about …' Nevertheless, every year many candidates assume that it is just that. Here are some hints to help you to understand how to answer the question that has been set.

| | |
|---|---|
| *Discutez* | This often follows a direct quotation. There is likely to be more than one viewpoint on the subject, and you should consider them both (or all). |
| *Dans quelle mesure …* | 'To what extent?' You will probably agree with the question up to a point, but not entirely; explain how far you go along with it and why you go no further. |
| *A quel point …?* | This means the same as *dans quelle mesure*?. It does **not** mean 'at what point in the play/novel?'. |
| *Croyez-vous …?* | You will probably have to put both sides of the question, but come to a decision at the end. |
| *Est-ce qu'il vous semble …?* | As above. |
| *Comparez* | The essay will need to be balanced between the two elements or attitudes you are comparing. It may include an element of contrast. |
| *Faites le contraste* | You should concentrate on the opposing viewpoints. |
| *Choisissez* | Select carefully. Check precisely what, who or how many you have to choose and pick examples that fit the particular aspect you are asked to deal with. |

*Letts*
Q&A

| | |
|---|---|
| *Que pensez-vous de ...?* | It's important to make this a personal response, but even so you must refer closely to the text or topic. |
| *Considérez ... du point de vue de ...* | Don't just 'consider' it, make sure you do so from the point of view specified. |
| *Analysez, Commentez, Etudiez, Examinez, Expliquez* | All require you to consider a certain aspect in detail and to comment on it. |
| *Justifiez* | It is particularly important to relate your comments to the text or give precise examples to illustrate your point of view. |
| *Dans quel sens ...?* | 'In what sense?' This means that the statement being made is certainly true, but probably only in one particular way. You have to decide what that way is. |
| *Evaluez* | Comment on the importance of the aspect being discussed. |
| *Comment ...?* | 'How?', 'In what way?'. This often relates to style, e.g. *Comment est-ce que l'auteur nous révèle le caractère de ...?* |
| *Imaginez* | Prepare to put yourself into a particular role; work out precisely what you are being asked to do and think what tone you need to adopt in order to fulfil the task (for more hints on this, see the comments on the sample essay on *Une région de la France*). |

It is often helpful, once you have decided which subject you are going to tackle, to highlight on the paper the key words in the question; for example, taking the essay on *Le Tartuffe* below, you would highlight *Evaluez l'importance, rôle* and *Elmire*.

## WHAT TO REVISE

### Useful constructions

Don't be put off if you don't know, or are not sure how to use, some of these expressions. Decide what level of language you are aiming at; you may be happy to keep your writing simple and concentrate on the ideas you put into your essay. Remember also that if you use a difficult construction incorrectly you won't gain the credit for using it in the first place and you may even lose marks because your meaning is not clear.

- Subjunctives
- Compound tenses (pluperfect, future perfect, conditional perfect)
- Passives
- Constructions with the infinitive
- *Après avoir/être* + past participle
- *En* + present participle
  (Remember that the last two must refer to the subject of the main verb.)
- Agreement of the past participle with a preceding direct object
- *Depuis* + present or imperfect tense
- Pronouns (direct and indirect object, *y, en*) – but get their position right.
- *Qui, que, dont*
- *Ce qui, ce que, ce dont*

- *Celui, celle, ceux, celles*
- *Lequel, laquelle, lesquels, lesquelles* (also after preposition)
- Correct word order (e.g. adverb straight after verb)
- Negatives (don't just stick to *ne … pas*)

There are many more; make your own list of interesting expressions as you come across them during the course of your reading.

## Mistakes to avoid

Be particularly careful about verb endings, singular and plural endings of nouns, agreement of adjectives, wrong genders (particularly of obvious words such as *la femme*), accents that change the meaning. Look through your past essays and see what mistakes you have made; examine them closely, work out what you did wrong and, if possible, why. Then look up in a grammar book or in a revision guide the appropriate points and learn them. There is never any excuse for making the same mistake twice!

# SAMPLE QUESTIONS AND ANSWERS

## General essay

This does not usually figure as part of the Topic paper, but is either a separate unit or part of a Mixed Skills module. Not all Boards include it in their syllabus.

The subject matter is likely to be a matter of general interest which is not specifically related to France or a Francophone country. You may have to write your essay 'off-the-cuff', (not literally, of course, as this would count as unfair practice and you would be excluded from the examination!) or you may have been given advance information about the general subject area to enable you to do your own research on the topic. Whichever is the case, you can help yourself by keeping up to date with what is happening around you, by reading newspapers and watching current affairs programmes on television and by discussing what you have read and heard with your friends. Approximately half of the marks for this essay will be allocated for the content, and the other half for the standard of your written French.

**TASK A** *Les problèmes du chômage*

**ANSWER**

De nos jours le taux de chômage tend à augmenter. En Angleterre il y a entre 2,5 et 3 millions de chômeurs, pour des raisons diverses; quelques-uns ont perdu leur emploi quand la compagnie pour laquelle ils travaillaient a fait faillite, d'autres parce que l'entreprise a voulu fermer une succursale, d'autres (par exemple des gradués) parce qu'ils n'ont pas réussi à être embauchés après leur période de formation. Quelle que soit la raison, tout le monde doit accepter que de graves problèmes en résultent.

Ces problèmes sont de deux genres: financiers et mentaux. Il est difficile de décider quel aspect est le plus dur à supporter.

Examinons d'abord les difficultés que suscite un manque d'argent. Comment est-ce qu'on peut continuer à payer les frais quotidiens d'une famille? J'ai un ami dont le père a été licencié; ils essaient de vendre leur maison et ils ont l'intention de déménager à un petit appartement afin de faire des économies. Mais ils ont toujours besoin de nourriture et de vêtements, et mon ami et sa soeur doivent se passer de choses 'de luxe' comme par exemple les visites aux discos, les cassettes et les magazines.

Mais il y a aussi le revers de la médaille. Il me semble que les chômeurs doivent faire face à des problèmes internes. Ils ont tendance à penser qu'ils sont sans valeur, que personne ne se soucie d'eux. Certains commencent à se lever tard, à passer leur temps couché sur le canapé du salon à regarder la télé, à croire que ça ne vaut pas la peine de chercher un autre poste. Cette situation peut devenir difficile pour leur famille, qui veut les encourager et qui n'aime pas cette réaction. Il faut les convaincre que bien qu'ils soient provisoirement sans emploi, ils ne doivent pas perdre tout espoir.

Il serait trop facile de dire qu'on devrait faire quelque chose pour rectifier la situation. S'il y avait des solutions faciles, on les aurait déjà trouvées. Mais je crois que le gouvernement devrait essayer de créer plus d'emplois à court terme, surtout pour ceux qui n'ont jamais travaillé. Je pense aussi qu'on devrait ouvrir des centres où les chômeurs pourraient aller pendant la journée, pour qu'ils puissent rencontrer des gens qui ont les mêmes problèmes et afin qu'ils ne se sentent plus seuls.

Not all Boards require you to study literature. For many it is an option, as an alternative to other cultural themes (such as the French Cinema or Impressionism) or to a non-literary topic such as '*La condition féminine*', '*la violence*', '*La France sous l'Occupation*', ecology, transport, or the detailed study of an area of France.

If you are studying French literature there are several 'prescriptions' available, which again depend on the particular Board for whose examinations you are being prepared.

❶ A list may be provided from which a specific text or texts must be chosen and studied in detail.

❷ A theme (e.g. *l'Enfance et l'Adolescence, La Guerre, La Société*) may be studied with relation to specific texts.

❸ A theme may be studied and related to any appropriate text or texts; this effectively leaves the choice of book, play etc. to the school.

Most new syllabuses now expect you to write your essays in French, but some say that they may be written in English. The required length also varies. There is therefore a very wide range of options available, and as in the three other aspects of the examination you must be absolutely clear about what you actually have to do. In the following pages you will find an example of each of the types of essay that you may be called upon to write, together with some hints on how best to approach them.

### A straightforward essay in English on a prescribed set text

*Colette: Le Blé en Herbe* – Discuss the character of Phil

In 'Le Ble en Herbe' we see Phil as a young man in the throes of adolescence, caught between two opposing forces: his love for his childhood friend Vinca and his awakening need for physical fulfilment. His problems are caused by the conflict between the two sides of his nature.

First and foremost he is a young man on the threshold of manhood, impatient for time to pass. He is reaching physical maturity before Vinca, and this has caused friction – or at least uneasiness – between two young people who were formerly closely attuned to each other and in some way apart from the rest of the world, even from their parents. A constraint has come into their relationship, the constraint that comes when a boy and girl become aware of each other's, and their own, sexuality. Phil is a young man 'né pour la chasse et la tromperie'; although at the outset he does not look upon Vinca as a target for his physical yearnings he is still possessive about her.

At times, however, he is still a child, with a boy's delight in shrimping and swimming. He finds it hard to come to terms with the two sides of himself. This causes him to speak sharply to Vinca and to inflict pain upon her by his thoughtlessness. His confusion brings unhappiness to them both.

Yet there is little doubt that Phil genuinely loves Vinca – a love that is expressed by implication rather than in words. They have discussed their future together and wisely decided that there is no point in telling their parents, who would tease them and not take their plans seriously. Phil has had to come to terms with the adults' lack of interest in him except on a purely superficial level.

The relationship between Phil and Vinca is so close that it comes as a shock to us to see Phil involved with another woman, despite his obvious desire to experience the pleasures of physical love. We cannot help but be disappointed in him and sorry for Vinca, though we can perhaps understand why he behaves as he does. Again we come up against the dichotomy in Phil's character; he loves Vinca deeply but not in a sexual way as yet, so his need for physical gratification must be satisfied elsewhere. He is always at risk from the machinations of a woman like Camille Dalleray; it is his misfortune, and Vinca's, that she appears on the scene at this particular time.

Whereas Phil is dominant in his relationship with Vinca, when we see him with Mme Dalleray he is quite different; clumsy and gauche. She plays on this – indeed, likes it – and it is at this point that Vinca appears to the reader to be the more mature of the two. Despite his initiation into manhood, Phil's reactions are often childish, showing once again the conflict within himself. He believes that he can keep the two women quite separate in his life; Mme Dalleray is aware that she cannot break down the barrier between them that is formed by Phil's feelings for Vinca. Here he is loyal to his first love, and he goes some way towards redeeming himself in the reader's eyes. At the same time he cannot think of Vinca in the same terms as 'La dame en blanc' and from this point onwards shrinks from even the most casual physical contact with her. His love for Vinca must not be contaminated by the sensations aroused by Mme Dalleray which he recognises as being devoid of love.

It is perhaps inevitable that the cool, dark, sensuous atmosphere of the villa Ker-Anna should make a deep impression upon Phil. Red, black and gold hangings, velvet, silk, the scent of burning spices, all combine to create a unique ambiance which he will always associate with Mme Dalleray and which by its very exoticism is calculated to bind him to her. She succeeds in this so well that when his father mentions 'velours et soie' after Phil has received the message that she has gone, it is the final straw that breaks his spirit and he escapes from an unendurable situation by fainting.

His reaction to the news that she has left is more that of a child unexpectedly denied a looked-for treat than of the man he thinks he has become. He is trying to behave in a civilised fashion, taking refuge even in coarseness, but finally the effort is too much for him and having told himself 'J'y perds … quoi? – une nuit' he shouts aloud 'C'est cette nuit-là que je voulais, justement!'

Phil has changed as a result of his liaison with Mme. Dalleray. On the day following his first nocturnal visit to the villa he is unable to bear the sight of blood on Vinca's fishing-hook, or to accept her blithely stepping on a little crab. He has become more sensitive in some ways, yet at the same time less sensitive to the feelings of Vinca, for he seems unable to recognise that her cheerfulness is forced and that she is deeply unhappy. He is horrifed to discover eventually that she has known for some time about his new relationship; he has behaved selfishly and not considered the feelings of the one whom he professed to love.

Phil himself is responsible for the eventual destruction of the relationship as it existed previously between himself and Vinca. He knows that things will never again be the same – he thinks of them as 'un être qui fut Phil-et-Vinca'– though he would give a great deal to have everything back as it was. When, against his better judgment and yet unable to help himself, he is inveigled into a different kind of relationship with her, he is unhappy about it. At the end of the novel we are aware of his distress, which lies in his disappointment with himself, with Vinca, and with the ending of their idyll; for certainly they can never return to the old, easy footing. Phil has brought about the destruction of what was most dear to him, and the reader can only speculate how things will turn out for him in the future.

---

> **Examiner's commentary** This essay, which the candidate has chosen to write in English, is considerably longer than it would have been if it had been written in French. No word limit was specified, so the only constraint is one of time. It is, for the most part, relevant (see introductory notes on how to interpret essay titles). The candidate obviously knows the book well and has chosen her material carefully to illustrate the points she is making. There are one or two places where a quotation or a precise reference would have proved to the examiner that the candidate knows what she is talking about; in the second paragraph, for example, she could have quoted Phil's impassioned comments on '*patienter*', and when she refers to his awkwardness when he is with Camille Dalleray she could have referred to the incident with the thistles or to his clumsiness inside the villa. Otherwise this is a good essay and certainly answers the particular question that was set.

---

## A 'slanted' essay in French on a prescribed text

*Molière: Le Tartuffe – Evaluez l'importance du rôle d'Elvire*

A première vue le rôle d'Elvire ne semble pas très important. Les deux personnages principaux de la pièce sont, bien sûr, Tartuffe et Orgon; mais si on le considère de plus près on peut voir que Molière utilise Elvire à des fins spécifiques, et que c'est un personnage dont le rôle n'est pas négligeable.

Un aspect primordial de son rôle est le fait qu'elle révèle à Orgon la tromperie et l'hypocrisie de Tartuffe. Si on ne le détrompait pas, Orgon risquerait de perdre non seulement son argent et sa maison, mais aussi le respect de sa famille et de ses amis. Quelqu'un doit essayer de lui

**TASK C**

**ANSWER**

expliquer le vrai caractère de Tartuffe. La scène dans laquelle Elmire amène Tartuffe à lui parler de ses sentiments envers elle pendant qu'Orgon demeure caché sous la table est importante pour deux raisons: c'est une scène comique (parce que les spectateurs savent, bien sûr, qu'Orgon est là) et c'est une scène qui avance l'intrigue. Après cela, Orgon ne pourra plus fermer les yeux à l'hypocrisie de Tartuffe.

En agissant de cette façon, Elmire devient dans une certaine mesure le porte-parole de Molière; l'écrivain veut nous enseigner aussi bien que nous divertir. La situation découverte par Elmire montre aux spectateurs la tragédie éventuelle qu'entraîne l'obsession; c'est un thème auquel Molière revient dans presque toutes ses pièces.

Elmire dit plusieurs fois qu'elle n'aime pas 'faire l'éclat'. Elle préfère la vie calme, surtout dans son mariage. Nous devons donc comprendre qu'il vaut mieux tenir le beau milieu, être raisonnable, plutôt que d'aimer l'excès. Son rôle à cet égard n'est peut-être pas aussi important que celui de Cléante, mais il est néanmoins évident que Molière était convaincu de la vérité de ce point de vue. Dans toutes ses pièces il y a au moins un personnage qui représente 'la voix de la raison'.

Les 'féministes' du 20e siècle n'ont rien à voir aux spectateurs du 17 siècle; celles-là pourraient quand même trouver de quoi les satisfaire, parce que c'est à Elmire, la femme prudente, d'agir enfin pour détromper son mari qui, auparavant, ne se souciait point d'elle. De cette manière elle sert de contraste avec lui. Voilà un exemple du caractère universel du théâtre de Molière; ce qu'il a écrit peut s'appliquer aussi bien aux situations de nos jours.

A mon avis l'importance primordiale du rôle d'Elmire en ce qui concerne l'intrigue de cette pièce vient du fait que c'est elle qui révèle la vérité à Orgon, mais on doit se rappeler aussi qu'elle a quelque chose à nous montrer à propos du thème principal de l'oeuvre de Molière.

---

**Examiner's commentary**

This is not so straightforward a subject as the previous one. It is no longer 'Discuss the character of ...'; you have to evaluate the importance of the character's rôle. You may well need to refer to the character of Elmire, but the question is slanted so that you have firstly to consider what part she plays in the action and secondly to what extent and in what ways it is important.

The candidate has succeeded quite well in answering the question that has been set. She has made several valid points, including references to the main theme of Molière's plays – that obsession can lead to tragedy – and to the universal nature of his work, i.e. that because his plays are basically about human nature they can still be understood and enjoyed today. She could have related her comments more directly to the text; she has mentioned only one specific incident and there is only one brief quotation.

The reference she makes to feminists is, on the face of it, a dangerous one, but she has made it clear that she is not using the word in relation to the seventeenth century where it would be quite out of place, and the examiner might well be amused by this comment which shows that the candidate is prepared to give her own opinions even if they are not the traditional point of view.

Her use of language is sound rather than exciting; in places it is quite wordy ('*il est néanmoins évident que Molière était convaincu de la vérité de ce point de vue*'), and she has used no subjunctives or, indeed, very much in the way of complex structures. She could therefore expect to earn fairly good marks for her French and she would not score too highly for use of examples and illustration, but to compensate for this she might well pick up marks for the ideas she puts forward.

## Essays on a literature-related theme

The next two examples are in the form of plans rather than complete essays. They will give you some idea of how you might approach the subject. The introduction and conclusion are given in more detail to emphasise their importance.

*Les Mains Sales (Thème: L'engagement dans le théâtre de Sartre)*
*A votre avis, pourquoi Sartre a-t-il choisi 'Les Mains Sales' comme titre?*

**Introduction**  Avoir les mains sales, ça veut dire être engagé; qu'on s'implique dans une affaire, et qu'on n'hésite pas à accomplir des tâches illégales pour parvenir à ses buts. Si, oui ou non, il faut faire cela est un des problèmes que doit résoudre le 'héros' de la pièce, Hugo. On devrait considérer aussi les raisons pour lesquelles il veut se salir les mains, les idées des autres membres du parti communiste à cet égard, ce qu'il fait exactement et les conséquences de son acte.

1  Hugo veut se salir les mains – pourquoi?

2  Ce qu'il est chargé de faire par le Parti, et ce que les autres pensent de sa capacité de le faire. Est-ce que cela est significatif en ce qui concerne son caractère?

3  S'il y réussit: comment et pour quelles raisons? Est-ce qu'il en est satisfait?

4  Les conséquences, y compris le dénouement de la pièce. Qu'est-ce que Sartre semble vouloir nous dire?

5  La philosophie de Sartre – l'existentialisme. 'L'homme est la somme totale de ses actes'; il faut qu'il fasse toujours un choix, et 'se plonger dans la merde et le sang jusqu'aux coudes' pour en venir au but.

**Conclusion**  Le thème principal de la pièce, c'est comment et pourquoi Hugo réussit à tuer Hoederer – c'est-à-dire, qu'il arrive à avoir les mains sales – et le dilemme auquel il lui faut faire face. C'est sans doute pour cette raison que Sartre a donné à sa pièce le titre 'Les Mains Sales'.

---

*Beaumarchais: Le Mariage de Figaro* (Theme: Portrayal of society in literature)
*Quel tableau de la société l'auteur nous présente-t-il dans l'oeuvre que vous avez lue?*

**Introduction**  Beaumarchais a écrit Le Mariage de Figaro vers la fin du 18e siècle, à une époque où on commençait à prendre conscience d'une certaine malaise qui provenait des gens ordinaires et qui allait plus tard aboutir à la révolution française. Il est évident que Beaumarchais ne pouvait s'empêcher de donner sa propre opinion à l'égard des gens et des institutions qui méritaient d'être critiquées. Il prétendait qu'il visait celles de l'Espagne, non pas celles de la France; de cette façon il espérait éviter la censure. Tout en dépeignant les aspects de sa société qu'il n'aimait pas, il nous présente un tableau vivant des moeurs de l'époque.

1  L'aristocratie (le Comte, droit du seigneur, 'vous vous êtes donné la peine de naître, et rien de plus').

2  Situation des femmes (Marceline, la Comtesse, Suzanne).

3  Institutions: la loi – Brid'oison, beaucoup de procès.

4  La politique (réf. au monologue de Figaro – le savoir-faire vaut mieux que le savoir).

5  Autres problèmes: la censure, la médecine, l'armée etc.

**Conclusion** On peut facilement voir que la société telle que Beaumarchais nous la dépeint était prête à être réformée. Cette pièce prouve aussi que l'oeuvre d'un auteur reflète souvent l'époque dans laquelle il l'a écrite; ses idées viennent surtout de ce qu'il remarque dans sa vie quotidienne.

---

### An imaginative essay based on a non-literary topic

**TASK F**

*Une région de la France: la Normandie*
*Vous êtes agent immobilier. Ecrivez une lettre au directeur d'un collège britannique qui se demande s'il devrait acheter un château dans votre région. Vous devez le convaincre des avantages du projet pour ses élèves.*

**ANSWER**

Rouen, le 15 juillet

Monsieur

Vous avez l'occasion sans précédent d'acheter une des meilleures propriétés de notre région. Niché dans la verdure, entouré de petits villages pittoresques, le château de Grandespoir vous offre tout ce que vous pouvez désirer.

Laissons de côté le fait qu'il y a tant de chambres qui pourraient facilement être aménagées en dortoirs pour les élèves; oublions pour l'instant le plaisir qu'ils prendraient à goûter les spécialités normandes – escalopes de veau au calvados, tripes à la mode de Caen, tartes aux pommes; ne tenons aucun compte du cidre fermier qui serait à la disposition des professeurs, peut-être aussi aux élèves de terminale; réfléchissons plutôt aux avantages pédagogiques de ce projet. Vous ne pourriez trouver nulle part une région qui conforme mieux à vos besoins.

Vous y trouverez l'histoire: la tapisserie de la reine Mathilde à Bayeux qui dépeint la bataille de Hastings, le lieu à Rouen qui commémore la mort de Jeanne d'Arc, les plages du débarquement aux environs d'Arromanches qui rappellent les événements de la deuxième guerre mondiale. Trois endroits qui montrent les liens qui existent depuis des siècles entre nos deux pays.

Vous y trouverez la culture: marchez dans les pas de Maupassant et de Flaubert, suivez la route prise par le fiacre d'Emma Bovary. Visitez les musées de Beaux-arts et de Normandie dans l'enceinte du château à Caen, admirez la dentelle dans le musée Baron Gérard à Bayeux et l'architecture merveilleuse des cathédrales. Assistez aux concerts donnés dans nos églises par des chorales qui viennent de tous les coins du monde.

Vous y trouverez la détente: de belles plages sont à portée, on peut se baigner dans la mer, voir les petits ports de pêche, faire la planche à voile, visiter les haras, faire de l'équitation. Les jardins de Normandie sont merveilleux aussi, dont le plus célèbre, celui de Monet à Giverny, vous inspirera un sentiment de paix avec ses nénuphars et son pont japonais. Que demander plus?

Et enfin, vos élèves apprendront à parler couramment le français, en écoutant la langue de première main. Cette expérience leur donnera un amour pour la Normandie et pour la France dont ils ne voudront jamais se débarrasser. Quand ils seront plus âgés ils pourront se servir de leurs connaissances pour trouver un emploi en Europe.

N'hésitez pas, Monsieur! Profitez du prix intéressant qui vous est proposé. Vous n'aurez jamais de regrets.

Je vous prie d'agréer, Monsieur, l'expression de mes sentiments les meilleurs.

**Examiner's commentary** This is a good response to the task. The candidate has put himself in the position of the estate agent, starting and ending with a reference to the property, its position and its price. The main body of the letter is packed with precise information about the area which is geared specifically towards the educational advantages to be gained by the pupils together with a few tantalising comments to lure the teachers as well. His enthusiasm for the area, both as 'estate agent' and candidate, is obvious, and it would be a very strong-minded headmaster who would throw this letter in the waste-paper basket without giving the matter further consideration. We might even speculate that the candidate has chosen the date deliberately to coincide with the end of term so that the headmaster is able to visit the site and see for himself.

The letter is well constructed, and the vocabulary is appropriate to the subject-matter. If we were looking for faults we might notice the change of tense from the conditional to the future, though that might have been intentional; there is no subjunctive, but in a task of this type it is not always easy to include one.

Provided it is within the word limit allowed, it would almost certainly score highly. It proves that if you know a good deal about a subject you are likely to write well about it.

Many people decide that they are not going to choose to do an imaginative essay because they feel that it isn't the sort of thing they do well. This may indeed be the case; but don't make up your mind until you have tried at least one during the course of your A-level studies. You might surprise yourself.

## SAMPLE QUESTIONS AND ANSWERS

For Mixed Skills questions, find out precisely what is stated in your syllabus and see if you can work out what range of exercise types might be used. You will find below some examples of tasks that could be set; but do not fall into the trap of thinking that they are the only possible tasks. As your Exam Board's papers become available, look at the material in this book and try using it also as a basis for the tasks that have actually been set.

### Listening and Writing

**Messages au répondeur**

(You will find two messages recorded after Listening Task O on the CD/cassette)

Telephone messages are notoriously difficult to understand in any language. Don't panic if you can't make out what is being said at first; there is, after all, a written stimulus (see below) which should help you with certain words.

Listen to the first message several times. If you still can't glean enough from it to be able to complete the task, **as a last resort** look at the text of the message which is printed at the end of the three Listening and Writing tasks, on p.96.

**TASK A**

> ### CALLIPURDY ASSOCIATES
> Plastic box storage system
> Suitable for homes and offices
> Various colours available
> Small, medium, large
> Discount available on large purchases
> Speedy delivery U.K. and abroad

Ecrivez le texte du fax que vous allez envoyer à M. Henri Dutertre des Etablissements Dufico. Vous devez lui donner tous les détails qu'il a demandés. Utilisez l'annonce ci-dessus pour vous aider.

## FAX

A l'attention de:   M. Henri Dutertre, Etablissements Dufico

De la part de:     Callipurdy Associates

Date:           le 8 mars 1996

Monsieur

Systèmes de rangement Callipurdy

Nos boîtes en plastique conviennent également aux bureaux et à la maison. On peut y ranger des affaires de toutes sortes: papiers, dossiers, livres, jouets etc.

Les couleurs disponibles sont rouge, gris, beige, bleu et vert.

Les petites (40cm × 35cm × 25cm) sont à 46f
Les moyennes (50cm × 35cm × 25cm) sont à 63f
Les grandes (65cm × 45cm × 40cm) sont à 85f

Si vous achetez vingt articles ou plus, de n'importe quelle taille ou couleur, nous pouvons vous donner un rabais de 10%.

A la suite de la réception de votre commande, la livraison est garantie en moins de cinq jours, même pour la France.

Veuillez agréer, Monsieur, l'expression de nos sentiments distingués.

---

**Examiner's commentary**  It is unlikely that in an exercise of this type many marks would be available for complexity of language; 'conveying the message' is the main objective, and accuracy of language is also important. This example shows that it is possible to write in a work-related context without using a huge range of business vocabulary. If you have to deal with this type of task, some topic-specific words are useful (*la commande, la livraison, le rabais* etc); you will certainly have learnt these if your syllabus requires them.

This example is about 100 words long. It conveys all the information that is asked for, and there is no need to pad it out any further.

---

Ecrivez une lettre en réponse au deuxième message de la part de M. Dutertre.

**Examiner's tip**  This is a more open-ended task as it leaves you to decide how to deal with the client and whether or not to accept that the error is yours. Nevertheless you should answer all the points raised in the telephone message.

**ANSWER**

Callipurdy Associates
Waringford
WF 35 1JD

M. Henri Dutertre
Etablissements Dufico
Vieilleville
France

le 18 avril 1996

Monsieur

Je regrette infiniment les erreurs que vous avez trouvées dans notre facture. Malheureusement, l'employée qui s'occupait de votre commande est malade et son remplaçant n'avait pas pu en trouver tous les détails.

Je peux confirmer que le prix des articles est comme convenu; en fait il a augmenté à partir du premier avril, mais puisque nous avons reçu votre commande le 15 mars il n'y a pas de problème. Le montant reste celui que nous vous avions déjà proposé.

Quant aux boîtes qui manquaient, j'espère que vous les avez maintenant reçues. Nous avions dû attendre un nouveau lot de rouges, parce que c'est un coloris très populaire. Veuillez nous faire savoir tout de suite si elles ne sont pas encore arrivées.

Nous vous prions d'agréer, Monsieur, l'expression de nos sentiments distingués.

---

**Examiner's tip** The Exam Board may state in the syllabus that it will print the beginning and ending of the letter on the paper for you. If this is not the case, be sure to revise the appropriate formal phrases; you probably learned them for GCSE, so they will not be unfamiliar to you.

---

**Examiner's commentary** In this example, which is about 120 words long, the vocabulary used is still quite straightforward; if the candidate had not known *facture* already it could have been taken from the telephone message. *montant* and *lot* are specific, but it would have been possible to express them more simply (e.g. *la somme totale, des boîtes rouges*). As this is a letter rather than a fax the candidate has taken the opportunity to use a range of language that is more complex: there are two examples of the agreement of the past participle with a preceding direct object, *celui que, quant à*, two examples of the pluperfect tense, the pronoun *en*, and the formal *veuillez nous faire savoir*.

---

**Examiner's tip** In both these tasks, as with any writing exercise which requires you to include certain specific details, it is a good idea to tick off on your paper each point as you answer it. Marks will certainly be allocated for the transmission of particular points, and you will lose them if you omit any of the details you have been asked to give.

---

## Salon de l'Auto à Bruxelles

TASK C

ANSWER

*Après avoir visité le Salon de l'Auto à Bruxelles vous écrivez un article (180 mots environ) pour le journal de votre collège, dans lequel vous résumez vos impressions de ce que vous avez vu et vos opinions de ce dont vous avez entendu parler.*

Les visiteurs sont venus en masse assister au Salon de l'Auto à Bruxelles. Il y avait des gens qui se bousculaient pour voir leurs marques préférées, d'autres qui voulaient s'y asseoir, d'autres encore qui se faisaient une collection de catalogues, même quelques-uns – minoritaires, à mon avis – qui avaient l'intention de s'offrir une nouvelle voiture.

La question qui se posait partout, c'était celle du diesel: pour ou contre? On dit que les voitures diesel se vendent beaucoup plus en Belgique que celles qui ont le moteur à essence. Il faut néanmoins accepter que certains n'aiment pas l'odeur de ce carburant; en revanche on pourrait dire que le prix plus bas est un facteur considérable. Il y a 9f de différence actuellement avec l'essence sans plomb, et plus de 11f avec la super plombée.

Pourtant certains vendeurs se plaignent qu'une nouvelle taxe dite 'compensatoire' ait été décidée, qui va augmenter les frais de circulation pour ceux qui ont une voiture diesel. Ces vendeurs ont peur que cela ne détourne les acheteurs éventuels.

Quant à moi, je trouve que la question de la pollution est encore plus importante que celle du prix du carburant; après avoir pesé le pour et le contre je suis d'avis que la sans-plomb est toujours meilleure pour l'environnement.

---

**Examiner's commentary**   Boards vary widely in the number of words they suggest for an exercise of this type. You may have to write as few as 100 or as many as 180. Usually the length of the stimulus material will be the determining factor; the more items of information there are to convey, the more words you are likely to be allowed. Nevertheless, you may not be expected to include all the possible points; look at the mark allocation before you start.

Marks are often awarded for an appropriate response to the task; in this example you are asked to write an article for a school newspaper, so you will need to think about the tone you are going to adopt as well as covering the aspects required (your impressions and your opinions). The candidate here has succeeded quite well in fulfilling the task, though she could have made more reference to the 'school newspaper' element (e.g. was it a school trip?) She may have decided not to include this as she is already a little over the limit of 180 words.

There are several examples of good use of language for which credit would be gained:

1 Interesting vocabulary – *sont venus en masse, se bousculaient, minoritaires, se plaignent* (rather than the simple *dire*) among others. She has borrowed some words from the passage, but that is probably acceptable as it is a Listening text and she has transcribed them correctly.

2 'Faux amis' used properly – *assister aux, actuellement, éventuels.*

3 Infinitive constructions – '*voulaient s'y asseoir*' (also good use of the pronoun), *avaient l'intention de s'offrir.*

4 Use of reflexive verbs to express the passive – *la question qui se posait partout, les voitures diesel se vendent beaucoup plus.*

5 Use of *on dit que.*

6 Use of the subjunctive – *se plaignent qu'une nouvelle taxe ... ait été décidée, ont peur que cela ne détourne.*

7 Use of *celle(s)* and *ceux.*

8 Good linking phrases – *en revanche, quant à moi, je pense que ...* (N.B. this is not the same as *à mon avis je pense que*, which says the same thing twice), *après avoir pesé le pour et le contre.*

(There is a danger with the last example that having learned the phrase you are determined to put it in to your essay regardless of whether it is really appropriate. On this occasion it certainly makes good sense, though if the candidate felt that she needed to cut down her words it could be omitted.)

**Text of answerphone messages**

**A**

C'est de la part de M. Henri Dutertre, Etablissements Dufico.

Je suis sa secrétaire.

Il a entendu parler de vos produits, et il voudrait en avoir plus de détails: par exemple les modèles et les couleurs possibles, les prix, quel rabais vous pouvez lui proposer, et les délais de livraison.

Vous pouvez nous contacter par fax: le numéro est 99 35 66 17.

**B**

Nous venons de recevoir votre facture et il nous semble qu'il y a plusieurs erreurs dedans.

Le prix est trop élevé et le rabais convenu n'apparaît pas sur la facture. De plus, quand nous avons reçu les marchandises quatre articles manquaient.

Voulez-vous vérifier les détails, s'il vous plaît, et nous faire savoir aussitôt que possible ce que vous allez faire pour rectifier la situation.

## Reading and Writing

**TASK D**

*Vous avez décidé de poser votre candidature pour le poste F. Ecrivez le texte de votre lettre.*
[Refer to the stimulus material for Task B in the Reading section.]

**ANSWER**

Monsieur

J'ai lu votre annonce dans le journal du 6 décembre et je vous écris pour poser ma candidature pour le poste dans la section sport du CISM.

J'ai 27 ans; je suis gradué en informatique de l'université de Londres, et je m'y connais à tous les aspects des ordinateurs. Je me suis spécialisé dans les systèmes de gestion de données.

Quant aux sports, j'ai fait partie des équipes de rugby, de hockey et de tennis à l'université, et à l'âge de 18 ans j'ai été sélectionné pour l'équipe nationale de rugby des moins de 21 ans. Je suis membre d'une équipe à Londres.

Je suis bilingue: mon père est anglais et ma mère est française. Chaque année je passe les vacances chez mes grands-parents qui habitent à Morzine. Je fais régulièrement du ski.

Je m'intéresse énormément à ce poste; je crois que mes connaissances en informatique alliées à mes talents dans le domaine des sports vous seraient utiles. Je suis sûr que je pourrais réussir aux tâches, quelles qu'elles soient, que vous me proposeriez.

Veuillez agréer, Monsieur, l'expression de mes sentiments distingués.

**Examiner's commentary** We are assuming that as you are asked to write only the text of the letter there is no need to include addresses and signature.

This letter is probably written tongue-in-cheek; the candidate has made up details that would be likely to attract the attention of the person reading the application and he does not suffer from false modesty. Nevertheless it is a good response to the task; he has used the stimulus material well and it would gain high marks from the point of view of content. There is some complexity of language; the examiner would probably not take *poser ma candidature* into account as it is in the question itself, but phrases such as *je m'y connais*, and *systèmes de*

*gestion de données* would gain credit. He has used a passive verb (*j'ai été sélectionné*), and has managed to include a subjunctive (*quelles qu'elles soient*) towards the end.

Now try writing similar letters of application for some of the other posts on the page. It doesn't matter if they are jobs which would not suit you; you need to be able to pick out from the stimulus the points that need to be answered. It will also give you practice in using your imagination.

*Lisez la réclame 'La magie des rencontres'. Utilisez l'information que vous y trouvez pour écrire un compte rendu des vacances que vous avez prises.* [Refer to the stimulus material for Task E in the Reading section.]

**TASK E**

**ANSWER**

Je viens de passer des vacances inoubliables au Japon. La compagnie Explorator, qui a organisé le séjour, a fait tout ce qui était nécessaire pour assurer notre confort.

Quant au pays, quelle diversité, et quel contraste! Après avoir quitté les rues de Tokyo pleines d'employés de compagnies, nous avons voyagé en car pour pénétrer en plein coeur du pays. Dans les champs, des paysans solitaires travaillaient à cultiver le riz. Partout, dans les villages que nous avons traversés, des poissons en plastique flottaient devant les maisons pour célébrer la fête des garçons. Le mont Fuji, couronné de neige, m'a surtout attiré; en descendant par les routes tortueuses nous avons remarqué des singes sauvages. Un jour, nous avons visité les ateliers des artisans traditionnels; j'aurais voulu acheter une canne à pêche, mais j'ai cru qu'il serait difficile de la porter.

La veille de notre retour, nous avons assisté à une 'cérémonie de thé'. Une Japonaise, en kimono brodé d'or, nous a servi du thé parfumé. C'est un moment dont je me souviendrai toujours.

De retour maintenant je trouve difficile d'imaginer que j'étais à 22 000 km de l'Angleterre. Mais voilà, n'est-ce pas, la raison pour laquelle on prend les vacances?

**Examiner's commentary** Here the choice of destination has been left to the candidate. She has no way of knowing whether the company concerned organises trips to Japan, but it does not matter. She has clearly chosen to write about a place she has visited; this is wise, because with very few exceptions people write best about something they know.

More important still is the fact that she has selected her material with care; she has not lost sight of the fact that her answer must be based on the stimulus material. She has therefore chosen details that illustrate the *beauté du paysage* (Mount Fuji), the *rare équilibre entre les hommes, la nature et les sites* (people working in the paddyfields) and the *instants uniques* (the tea ceremony). She has also referred to the good organisation of the trip.

She would score high marks for content and response to the task. Her use of vocabulary is good: for example *pénétrer en plein coeur du pays, couronné de neige, les routes tortueuses.* Many of her constructions are interesting: *tout ce qui était nécessaire, après avoir quitté, en descendant, j'aurais voulu acheter, nous a servi du thé, dont je me souviendrai toujours.*

There are, however, a few places where her French is not entirely clear (*quel contraste* – what precisely is being contrasted? Are the plastic fish celebrating the boys' festival, or is it the inhabitants? What exactly does the final sentence mean? – at first sight it looks impressive, but it doesn't really say anything. There are some other awkward patches: *J'ai cru qu'il serait difficile de la porter* could have been more neatly expressed, and she gives the impression that she was determined to use the direct object pronoun at all costs in this sentence.

The overall impression is still that this is a good quality answer.

*Letts*
**Q&A**

You may have to write a summary in French, using your own words. Even if your Board does not require this, it is a useful exercise as it gives you practice in picking out the important points from a text and expressing it in different terms.

**TASK F** *Ecrivez en français un résumé de l'article. N'oubliez pas d'utiliser vos propres termes; vous n'avez pas le droit de copier de longues sections du texte.* [This task refers to the following article.]

**ENTREPRISES**

## CHERCHEZ LA FEMME

« Interdit aux chiens et aux femmes. » La règle officiellement en vigueur dans les très sélects clubs anglais s'applique également – mais plus sournoisement – à la

*Isabelle Bouillot*

tête des grandes entreprises françaises. Une récente étude du cabinet de recrutement Boyden, publiée par *La Lettre des états-majors*, le démontre, chiffres à l'appui.

Dans les 200 plus grands groupes français, seuls 4 % des postes de direction sont occupés par des représentantes du sexe dit faible. Plus de la moitié de ces directeurs en jupon restent d'ailleurs cantonnés dans le ghetto de la communication et des ressources humaines. Des fonctions où leurs qualités purement féminines font des miracles, a-t-on coutume d'expliquer dans les états majors. Explication typiquement phallocrate. « *Ces activités ont surtout un faible potentiel de pouvoir* », remarque Bénédicte Bertin-Mourot, coresponsable de l'Observatoire des dirigeants au CNRS. Les DRH et les « dircoms » prennent rarement part aux comités stratégiques. Et ce ne sont pas vers ces postes que l'on regarde lorsqu'un poste de directeur général est à pourvoir. Depuis Yvette Chassagne, qui a dirigé l'UAP de 1983 à 1987, plus aucune femme n'est parvenue à la tête d'une « major ».

Les femmes d'affaires sont encore moins bien accueillies dans les conseils d'administration. Sur un total de 2 261 mandats d'administrateur, elles ne s'en partagent que 58 (hors représentants du personnel). Loin de donner l'exemple, le secteur public se montre encore plus misogyne que le privé. Les rares administrateurs femmes de l'Etat-entreprise se recrutent chez les surdouées de la haute fonction publique, comme Isabelle Bouillot. Après avoir défrayé la chronique en devenant la première femme directrice du Budget, elle fut admise à trois conseils (EDF, La Poste et la Seita).

Dans le privé, la meilleure façon de pénétrer le bastion du pouvoir mâle reste la voie familiale. Si Monique n'était pas la veuve de Francis, siégerait-elle au conseil du groupe Bouygues? Même question pour Liliane Bettencourt, fille du fondateur, à L'Oréal. Et même l'émérite Elisabeth Badinter, grande prêtresse de l'égalité des sexes, doit son siège d'administrateur de Publicis à son père, Marcel Bleustein-Blanchet, fondateur du groupe. ∎

**OLIVIER TOSCER**

For marking purposes this passage might be divided into roughly 20 sections as shown below, or a global mark out of 20 might be awarded to take into account the overall impression given by the candidate's French.

*Une enquête menée par une organisation chargée de la recherche du personnel/a découvert que les femmes n'atteignent que rarement/le niveau de direction/dans les grandes compagnies en France./ Dans les entreprises où l'on trouve des 'femmes-directeurs'/elles doivent souvent se contenter/de la responsabilité des domaines dits 'féminins';/ elles doivent s'occuper de la communication et du personnel./ C'est une attitude chauvine,/ surtout parce que les gens qui ont des responsabilités de ce genre/n'ont pas souvent le droit de prendre des décisions importantes,/ et la promotion au poste de PDG/ne vient que rarement de ces rangs./ Le pourcentage est encore plus petit/à ce niveau-là dans l'administration;/ on entend parler partout de celles qui y parviennent/parce qu'elles sont rares./ Dans le secteur privé/il est plus facile d'obtenir un poste de ce genre/si l'on est apparenté à quelqu'un qui a déjà des liens avec l'entreprise dont il s'agit./*

---

**Examiner's tip**  Here you are able to use some of the vocabulary from the passage. The important thing, again, is to select your material carefully; you should make a note of the main points of the text and then put them into your own words. If you are allowed to use a monolingual dictionary you will be able to find synonyms for some of the words; if you then look carefully to see how these new words are used by studying the examples given, you may find further expressions that will fit in well with your summary.

For example: look up *étude*; you may find *enquête*. Look up *enquête*, and you may find *mener* used with it. Check *ressources* and you should find *ressources humaines* meaning *personnel*. Yet again the message is 'don't panic'. A text that looks at first to be impossible to understand, let alone to express in your own words, can be broken down into smaller bite-sized pieces that you will be able to cope with more confidently.

---

*Letts*
**Q&A**

# *Answers*

## LISTENING ANSWERS

| Task | | Answer | Mark |
|------|---|--------|------|
| A | 1 | b | 1 |
| | 2 | a | 1 |
| | 3 | b | 1 |
| | 4 | a | 1 |
| | 5 | c | 1 |
| | 6 | b | 1 |
| | 7 | b | 1 |

*Examiner's tip* Questions **6** and **7** require a basic knowledge of the geography of France. Did you remember that le Midi means the South of France, not the middle, and that the Pyrenees are in the SW, between France and Spain?

| Task | | Answer | Mark |
|------|---|--------|------|
| B | (a) | F | 1 |
| | (b) | V | 1 |
| | (c) | F | 1 |
| | (d) | F | 1 |
| | (e) | F | 1 |
| | (f) | V | 1 |
| | (g) | V | 1 |
| | (h) | F | 1 |
| | (i) | F | 1 |
| | (j) | F | 1 |
| | (k) | F | 1 |
| | (l) | F | 1 |
| | (m) | V | 1 |
| | (n) | F | 1 |
| | (o) | V | 1 |

*Examiner's tip* (a) Did you remember to check the tense?
(f) Remember that *vient de* + infinitive means 'has just'.
(j) *ne ... que* means 'only' and *au moins* is not the same as *moins de*.
(k) Check the tense again.
(n) *ne ... que* again.

C        (a)  défaites, Tricolores (ou Français), écossaise        3

| Task | Answer | Mark |
|------|--------|------|
| | (b) journée, 20h (8h du soir), Le Havre, 1–1 (un but partout) | 4 |
| | (c) gagnant, suisse | 2 |
| | (d) battu (ou éliminé), 40e (quarantième) | 2 |
| | (e) élire, députés, haute surveillance | 3 |
| | (f) Pape, d'état (ou officielle), 1959, quarante, fractures, défendre, manifesté | 7 |

**Examiner's tip** (a) If you wrote *Français* did you remember the capital letter because it is used as a noun?
*écossaise* has a small 'e' because it is being used as an adjective here.
(b) The name of the town is not *Havre*, but *Le Havre*. In the report *au Havre* was used because even in a place name you cannot say *à Le*.
(c) The report said *devant son public*, and the event was held in Switzerland.
(e) *députés* means 'members of parliament', not 'deputies'.
(f) *problèmes* would make sense (instead of *fractures*) but it is masculine so the adjective would have been *sociaux*.

| | | | | |
|---|---|---|---|---|
| **D** | **1** – (d) | **5** – (a) | | |
| | **2** – (i) | **6** – (h) | | |
| | **3** – (g) | **7** – (e) | | |
| | **4** – (b) | | | 7 |

| | | |
|---|---|---|
| **E** | (a) rappeler | 1 |
| | (b) son, goût | 2 |
| | (c) une bouteille d'encre | 1 |
| | (d) elle était jeune/enfant | 1 |
| | (e) mûres | 1 |
| | (f) aux genoux | 1 |
| | (g) aime | 1 |
| | (h) la pollution, l'odeur des tartines brûlées | 2 |

**Examiner's tip** (a) *souvenir* is not quite right as it does not fit correctly into the sentence you have been given, but you would probably gain the mark for comprehension.
(e) did you write *murs* and wonder why she was picking walls? A close look at your dictionary should have shown you the word for 'blackberries'.
(f) *au genou* in the singular would probably be accepted, but if you listen carefully to the passage you will hear the plural *les genoux*.
(g) the passage said *doit sa passion pour*; this would not fit into the sentence you have been given so you need to think what it actually means.

## Listening answers

| Task | | Answer | Mark |
|---|---|---|---|
| **F** | (a) | dans un lit (not *en voiture*) | 1 |
| | (b) | si vous arrivez tard (not *de bonne heure*) vous pouvez dîner (not *déjeuner*) | 2 |
| | (c) | ne paient rien (not *demi-tarif*) | 1 |
| | (d) | jusqu'au 30 juin minuit (not *à partir de*) | 1 |
| | (e) | 61 500 (not 71 500) | 1 |
| | (f) | L'offre n'est pas cumulable | 1 |
| | (g) | un fauteuil d'époque | 1 |
| | (h) | vous recevrez l'argent tout de suite/immédiatement | 1 |
| | (i) | on ne vous demande pas pourquoi vous voulez emprunter l'argent | 1 |
| | (j) | à l'heure du repas (not *quand il est temps de sortir*) | 1 |
| | (k) | des céréales et des viandes | 1 |
| | (l) | tendre ou moelleuse (not *dure*) | 1 |
| | (m) | repasser (not *laver*) | 1 |
| | (n) | selon le tissu (not *température*) | 1 |
| | (o) | la mère est plus enthousiaste que la fille (**or** la fille est moins enthousiaste que la mère) | 1 |
| | (p) | Concorde va fêter **or** fêtera demain, dimanche (not *a fêté hier*) | 1 |
| | (q) | deux billets, aller-retour Paris–New York | 2 |
| | (r) | on peut répondre maintenant aux questions (not *demain*) | 1 |

**Examiner's tip** (d) Look out for 'time' phrases and changes of tense. It's very easy to be misled by the date itself and not listen closely to what comes before or after it.

(g) *d'époque* means 'antique'; *d'occasion* is not the same. You didn't think *neuf* meant 'nine', did you? In that case it would have come before the noun.

(o) Although she says *ça me passionne* her tone of voice indicates the opposite. At this level you have to be able to draw conclusions from the way in which something is said, not just from the words themselves.

| Task | | Answer | Mark |
|---|---|---|---|
| **G(i)** | (a) | 2 | 1 |
| | (b) | 15h00 (**or** 3 heures de l'après-midi) | 1 |
| | (c) | 6000 | 1 |
| | (d) | 73000 | 1 |
| | (e) | 25% | 1 |
| | (f) | aucun (**or** nul **or** 0) | 1 |
| | (g) | un par heure | 1 |
| | (h) | demain | 1 |

| Task | Answer | Mark |
|------|--------|------|
| (i) mardi | | 1 |
| (j) depuis hier | | 1 |

(a) Did you notice the tense of the question? The passage said that this is the third day of the strike, so two days have already passed.

(b) Always make it clear whether you mean morning, afternoon or evening.

(d) Did you write 63 000? If you hear *soixante* don't write 60 until you have heard the rest of the number.

(e) This is not a maths examination, so 1/4 (*un sur quatre*) is likely to be accepted.

(g) *un* on its own would not be correct, as it does not answer the question.

(j) Be sure to write the whole of the answer here; *hier* alone is wrong.

**G(ii)** This is now the third day of strikes on the French railway system and talks are due to take place this afternoon. The dispute concerns a government scheme which the unions think would involve the closing of 6000 km of track and the loss of 73 000 jobs.

The situation is likely to be difficult for those travelling by train at the end of the weekend; on average, one train out of four is expected on the main lines. In the suburbs there will be no trains at all in or out of the *Gare de Lyon* or the *Gare du Nord*, one in four at the *Gare St Lazare* and the *Gare de l'Est*, one per hour at the *Gare d'Austerlitz* and the *Gare Montparnasse*. There are still problems on the express railway network (RER) in Paris on lines B, C and D, and there is a threat of disruption tomorrow on the Paris buses and underground as well.

In Rouen the situation has improved, as the seamen of two unions have lifted their blockade of one of the docks following a meeting with the port management.

**20**

There are several sets of initials in this passage (RER, CGT, CFDT). You will impress the examiner if you show that you know what they mean. They are often to be found in dictionaries, either in alphabetical order as usual or in a separate section. If you come across abbreviations of this type during the course of your studies, make a list of them as you go along.

| Task | Answer | Mark |
|------|--------|------|
| **H(i)** | **1** – (d) | 1 |
| | **2** – (e) | 1 |
| | **3** – (a) | 1 |
| | **4** – (f) | 1 |
| | **5** – (b) | 1 |

Listen very carefully to this exercise: many of the numbers are very similar.

| Task | Answer | Mark |
|------|--------|------|
| **H(ii)** | (a) protection (1) against severe paralysis (1) and even death (1) | 3 |

*Letts*
Q&A

| Task | Answer | Mark |
|------|--------|------|
| | (b) temples, stations, dispensaries, hospitals, pavements in poor districts, shanty towns | 6 |
| | (c) radio (1) television (1) press campaign (newspapers) (1) | 3 |
| | (d) It has always been amongst the leaders in such matters (1). General elections are not far away (1). | 2 |
| **I** | (a) 500 000. | |
| | (b) No need to leave the house (1); no specific timetables to keep to (1). | 2 |
| | (c) Lessons may arrive on computer disk (1) as well as in form of photocopied sheets (1) or books (1). | 3 |
| | (d) There are rules they have to obey (1); there is more competition (1). | 2 |
| | (e) The organisations responsible for paying various benefits (or ASSEDIC and ANPE) must have agreed (1) beforehand (1) that you can take this particular course (1). | 3 |
| | (f) 1f 29 per minute if you use Minitel. | 1 |

**Examiner's tip**

(b)/(c) Read all the questions before you start, so that you don't put the answer in the wrong place and then have to write it out again.

(e) It's not immediately obvious where the three marks are allocated here, so make sure you include all the details from the relevant sentence. In fact, *préalablement* (beforehand) is a vital part of the answer and is awarded one mark.

If you cannot identify a word even with the aid of a dictionary, consider whether the 'word' could in fact be a set of initials.

(f) You must put in 'per minute' or the answer is incorrect.

| Task | Answer | Mark |
|------|--------|------|
| **J** | (a) Deux mois. | 1 |
| | (b) Ils dresseront les plans des carrières. | 1 |
| | (c) Depuis le treizième siècle. | 1 |
| | (d) Des soldats britanniques (1) pendant la guerre de 14–18 (1). | 2 |
| | (e) A une profondeur de 20 m. | 1 |
| | (f) Afin que la séparation soit moins douloureuse. | 1 |
| | (g) Ils vont se passer de montres (1) et de radio (1). | 2 |
| | (h) Ils ont 400 litres d'eau pour l'hygiène. | 1 |
| | (i) Ils ont des boîtes de conserves (1) et d'aliments lyophilisés (1). | 2 |

**Examiner's tip**

(d) Did you answer both parts of the question?

(g) If a word you think you know appears not to make sense, check it to see if it has another meaning. Here, *se passer* has nothing to do with 'happen'; *se passer de* means 'to go without'.

| Task | Answer | Mark |
|------|--------|------|

Also check the mark allocation here: two marks are allowed, so it is likely to require only the two concrete items (watch and radio). If three marks had been indicated, you would have included *contact avec le jour*; in fact this might be acceptable anyway for one of the two marks.

| | | | |
|---|---|---|---|
| K | 1 | à l'occasion | 1 |
| | 2 | terminer | 1 |
| | 3 | d'ici quelques jours ('in a few days from now') | 1 |
| | 4 | atteindre | 1 |
| | 5 | décider | 1 |
| | 6 | risquent | 1 |
| | 7 | sauver | 1 |
| | 8 | composent | 1 |
| | 9 | rappellent | 1 |
| | 10 | au début | 1 |
| | 11 | perdre | 1 |
| | 12 | sont | 1 |

**Examiner's tip** If you look carefully at the words you have been given you will see that they fall into three categories: phrases involving time, verbs in the infinitive, and main verbs in the third person plural form (*ils/elles* ending). This will help you to eliminate several possibilities for each blank before you start.

**1** *lors de* is linked to *lorsque*, another word for 'when'.

**4** Did you realise that this was not *attendre*?

**5** 'to decide on' is *décider de*; this is why the pronoun is *en*.

**6** Not *sont*; this does not mean 'are sure of being made redundant', but 'are, of course, at risk of being made redundant'.

**8** Again, not *sont*; it would make better sense here than in **6**, but you need it later and you are allowed to use each word once only.

**10** *qu'* tells you that your chosen word must start with a vowel.

**12** *sont* – at last!

| | | | |
|---|---|---|---|
| L | 1 | Parce qu'on leur a interdit de vendre de l'alcool (1) la nuit (entre 21h du soir et 7h du matin) (1). | 2 |
| | 2 | Plusieurs centaines (**or** un millier). | 1 |
| | 3 | Parce que des gens qui ne sont pas 'comme il faut' viennent sur les lieux (1) et le risque de délinquance augmente à cause de ça (1). | 2 |
| | 4 | Ils ont refusé d'accepter les nouvelles règles (**or** personne n'a cessé de vendre l'alcool). | 1 |
| | 5 | Pour les habitants du quartier. | 1 |

| Task | | Answer | Mark |
|---|---|---|---|
| | 6 | On interdit aux petites épiceries du quartier de vendre de l'alcool (1) tandis que les bars restent ouverts très tard (1). | 2 |
| | 7 | A lutter (1) parce qu'ils veulent que l'interdiction soit retirée (1). | 2 |
| M | 1 | France is to end its nuclear tests (1) between now and the end of February (1). | 2 |
| | 2 | That we will: negotiate and work together (1); learn to speak to and listen to each other (1); try to understand that things change (1); and that ideas must also change (1). | 4 |
| | 3 | Negotiators who are sensible and responsible (1); a State which is ready to listen (1); strong trades unions (1); active and imaginative professional organisations (1). | 4 |
| | 4 | He is pleased with what the President has said (1) but is sceptical (1) because he wonders whether the Prime Minister feels the same way (1). | 3 |

**Examiner's tip** **2** This includes the idea of *dialogue social* and is stated more clearly, thus showing that you have understood the details.

| | | | |
|---|---|---|---|
| N | | Ten points, as shown below: | |
| | | There are economic reasons and sociological reasons. | 1 |
| | | The price of housing has gone up during the period under consideration. | 1 |
| | | There are now alternatives to investing in housing. | 1 |
| | | People are putting their money into life assurance | 1 |
| | | or investing it on the Stock Exchange (e.g. shares, bonds). | 1 |
| | | Households, particularly young couples, are finding it difficult to look forward to the future | 1 |
| | | because it seems to be unclear. | 1 |
| | | Family life in general is less stable. | 1 |
| | | Unemployment or the fear of it also puts people off buying their own home. | 1 |
| | | It is less important socially these days to own one's own home. | 1 |
| O | (a) | Il y a un psychologue scolaire à la disposition de toutes les écoles publiques maternelles et primaires (1). C'est-à-dire, un psychologue en moyenne pour 2000 élèves (1). | 2 |
| | (b) | Chercher à comprendre quels sont les problèmes psychologiques d'un élève (1) et en analyser les causes (1). | 2 |
| | (c) | Les psychologues scolaires travaillent d'une façon différente maintenant. | 1 |
| | | On concentre l'attention sur la communication | 1 |
| | | plutôt que sur l'échec. | 1 |
| | | Il faut absolument avoir la permission des parents d'un élève avant de lui parler, | 1 |

| Task | Answer | Mark |
|------|--------|------|
| | autrement on risque d'écarter sa confiance. | 1 |
| | Si l'enfant signale au psychologue un problème sérieux | 1 |
| | comme par exemple la violence physique ou sexuelle contre | |
| | un enfant de moins de 15 ans | 1 |
| | le psychologue doit absolument en parler aux autorités. | 1 |
| (d) | Avoir une licence de psychologie (1); être déjà enseignant de premier degré (1); suivre un cours de formation d'une année (1); dans un IUFM (1). | 4 |

**Examiner's tip** (d) If the passage has used a technical term (here *enseignant du premier degré*) you do not usually have to find another way of expressing it.

## READING ANSWERS

| Task | Answer | | Mark |
|------|--------|------|------|
| A | 1 V | 5 F | |
| | 2 F | 6 V | |
| | 3 V | 7 F | |
| | 4 F | 8 F | 8 |

**Examiner's tip**

**1** *l'étranger* = 'abroad', so is equivalent to *le monde entier*.

**2** This statement is correct until you reach the last word. In the advertisement it is *aviation **civile*** that is mentioned.

**3** *gyroscopique* gives you the meaning you need.

**4** A nice thought, but wrong! A telescopic aerial is by no means the same thing.

**5** An incorrect statement because it does not **only** work when plugged into the mains, it also works on batteries (*piles*).

**6** *micro* is short for *microphone*.

**7** *sangle*, not *sac*.

**8** A negative sentence; take extra care.

| Task | Answer | Mark |
|---|---|---|
| **B** | | |

|   | A | B | C | D | E | F | G | H |
|---|---|---|---|---|---|---|---|---|
| **1** | ✗ | ✗ | ✓ | ✗ | ✗ | ✗ | ✓ | ✗ |
| **2** | ✗ | ✗ | ✗ | ✓ | ✗ | ✗ | ✗ | ✗ |
| **3** | ✗ | ✗ | ✗ | ✓ | ✗ | ✓ | ✗ | ✗ |
| **4** | ✗ | ✗ | ✓ | ✓ | ✓ | ✓ | ✗ | ✗ |
| **5** | ✗ | ✗ | ✗ | ✗ | ✓ | ✗ | ✗ | ✗ |
| **6** | ✗ | ✓ | ✗ | ✗ | ✗ | ✗ | ✗ | ✓ |
| **7** | ✓ | ✗ | ✗ | ✗ | ✓ | ✗ | ✗ | ✓ |

**15**

**8** B     **1**

**9** G     **1**

**10** A     **1**

---

**Examiner's tip**    **1** *expert* can simply mean 'specialist'. Job **A** requires training + diploma **or** experience.
Job **C** – *chevronné*.
Job **E** – *ouvrier qualifié* is a skilled workman; this is not necessarily the same as experienced.

**2** Did you read the question carefully? It said *plus de deux*.

**3 D** – *traitement de texte* is 'word-processing', which could be counted as a branch of *informatique* (information technology).

**4 F** – has a **lower** age limit, but the question did not specify an **upper** limit.

**5** Although several others require a letter of application, with or without a CV, they do not insist that it is handwritten.

**8** *pédagogiques* gives it away, but even if you don't know the word the subject of encyclopaedias will help you to make a guess.

**10** *l'effet de serre* means 'greenhouse effect', but anyway the word *environnement* appears in the heading of the advertisement.

| Task | Answer | Mark |
|------|--------|------|

**C(i)**

|     | **Belges** | **Britanniques** | **Francais** |
|-----|:----------:|:----------------:|:------------:|
| (a) | ✓          |                  |              |
| (b) |            | ✓                |              |
| (c) | ✓          |                  |              |
| (d) | ✓          |                  |              |
| (e) |            | ✓                | ✓            |
| (f) |            | ✓                |              |
| (g) |            | ✓                |              |
| (h) |            |                  | ✓            |
| (i) |            |                  | ✓            |
| (j) | ✓          |                  |              |
| (k) | ✓          |                  |              |
| (l) |            | ✓                |              |

**13**

---

**Examiner's tip** (b) It is tempting to tick *Belges* for this one too, but read the paragraph carefully. The point being made is that the Belgians can easily travel to and from work in the capital; they do not therefore spend *beaucoup de temps* in doing so.

(c) *apprécie en connaisseur les bonnes choses de la vie.*

(d) (*il apprécie*) *la discipline dans le travail.*

(e) There are two separate paragraphs to refer to here: the two phrases that give you the answers are *beaucoup d'enfants la poursuivent jusqu'à 18 ans* and *Un jeune sur deux de 16 à 25 ans est scolarisé.*

(i) Remember *un tiers* is 'a third'. 30% is near enough.

(j) The key word here is *facilement.*

---

**C(ii)**    According to the magazine, the Belgians are individuals; for example, they prefer their houses not to be too similar. They enjoy the good things of life; they visit their favourite restaurants regularly. They do not like to give way on the roads, as the state of their cars – many of them are dented – proves. Nevertheless, they enjoy driving; many live in the suburbs or even in the country and use their cars to commute to work, which they can do easily as Brussels is small compared with London or Paris. A Belgian wife is likely to have her own car which she uses to ferry the children to and from school.

Belgians are hard-working and don't try to hide the fact. They know that by working hard they will earn the money to spend on the things

*Letts*
**Q&A**

| Task | Answer | | Mark |
|------|--------|---|------|

they enjoy. They are proud of their homes and of the well-being of their families.

There is little difference between the Belgians who live in the cities and those who live in the country or, despite what is often said, between those who live in the north and those who live in the south.

**20**

| D | 1 B | 4 A |
|---|-----|-----|
|   | 2 D | 5 F |
|   | 3 E | 6 C |

**Examiner's tip** Some of these are easily done: *manque* in **E** can be quickly matched with *omis* in **3**, for example. Others are less obvious and require real attention to detail. It is tempting to match **6** with **A** because the word *politiques* appears at the end of both, but **4** is closer to the sentiments expressed in the letter. The irritation of the writer could be said to show through in several of the letters, but the language of **F** is the strongest (*la prise en ôtage, abus, torpillage*). *déontologie* in **1** is not a word that comes obviously to mind; this would be unlikely to be set by a Board that did not allow the use of dictionaries.

| E | (a) | beaux (noun becomes adjective) | 1 |
|---|-----|-------------------------------|---|
|   | (b) | équilibrés (noun becomes participle) | 1 |
|   | (c) | connaît (noun becomes verb) | 1 |
|   | (d) | se déroulera (noun becomes verb) | 1 |
|   | (e) | envoyée (active verb becomes passive verb) | 1 |
|   | (f) | lisible (adverb becomes adjective) | 1 |
|   | (g) | ne sont pas vécus deux fois (or more simply, 'sont uniques') | 1 |
|   | (h) | ne sera nécessaire | 1 |
|   | (i) | dans notre brochure | 1 |

**Examiner's tip** d) Did you remember to use the reflexive form of the verb?

(e) Remember that the participle (*envoyée* – 'sent') in the passive should agree with the noun to which it refers.

(g) Revise the past participles of irregular verbs, especially those that you have learnt since starting your A-level course.

(h) *aucun* is the only negative that is actually an adjective. It still, of course, requires *ne*.

(i) You have to decide what the *y* stands for, and then remember that when you are no longer using a pronoun the phrase for which it stands has to be put in its normal position (i.e. no longer before the verb).

| Task | Answer | Mark |
|------|--------|------|
| **F(i)** | (a) 41 ans (1); garde du corps de François Santoni (1). | 2 |
| | (b) Il a été tué de plusieurs balles. | 1 |
| | (c) Devant une école (1) du quartier des Salines (1) à l'entrée sud d'Ajaccio (1). | 3 |
| | (d) Quelqu'un aurait voulu se venger d'un adversaire (1) ou se débarrasser d'un rivale politique (1) ou aurait tenté de régler une dispute en utilisant la violence (1). | 3 |
| | (e) 6 mois de prison (1) avec 4 mois de sursis (1). | 2 |
| | (f) Il a entamé un dialogue (1) avec tous les partis politiques (1). | 2 |
| | (g) Le FLNC-canal historique a cessé (1) provisoirement les attentats (1). | 2 |

**Examiner's tip**    In this type of exercise (and for this type of passage) it is not always easy to express the meaning in your own words. Try to do so if you can; it is possible to express something like *garde du corps* differently (*celui qui est chargé de protéger François Santoni contre des attentats éventuels*), but you may feel that nothing much is to be gained by doing so. Read the instructions at the beginning of the question on your paper carefully and see whether you are given any indication of how much, if anything, you are allowed to retain of the original.

(c) Check the number of marks available and make sure you find the right number of points.

(d) Remember that *éventuel* means 'possible', not 'eventual'.

(e) It is often difficult to explain legal terms in your own words. The first part of this is straightforward enough (*il doit rester incarcéré pendant six mois*) but most Boards would accept the use of *avec sursis*.

| Task | Answer | Mark |
|------|--------|------|
| **F(ii)** | (a) Le 16 février est l'anniversaire du jour (1) où J-P Leca a été tué (1). | 2 |
| | (b) Le FLNC-canal historique n'a jamais reconnu (1) sa culpabilité de cet assassinat (1). | 2 |
| | (c) Le processus politique qu'on a mis en train. | 1 |
| | (d) Ceux qui dirigent (1) la Cuncolta (1). | 2 |
| | (e) On devait (1) franchir un nouveau pas (1). | 2 |

**Examiner's tip**    Read the instructions carefully for this exercise. You may be required to use the word in brackets in exactly the form in which it is given or you may be expected to put it into the appropriate form. Either way this is a language-manipulation exercise and you will need to be very precise in your re-wording of the sentence. Usually it is possible to use some of the words that are in the original; if an example is provided, look at it carefully for clues.

| Task | Answer | Mark |
|------|--------|------|
| **G(i)** | (a) contant ses aventures outre-Atlantique | 1 |
| | (b) se creusent les méninges à la recherche de | 1 |
| | (c) dont la publication a fait grand bruit | 1 |

| Task | | Answer | Mark |
|------|------|--------|------|
| | (d) | suscitant bien des hommages | 1 |
| | (e) | donne chair et os | 1 |
| | (f) | à ses fidèles | 1 |
| | (g) | propre à enflammer | 1 |
| | (h) | à son effigie | 1 |
| | (i) | cet incroyable engouement | 1 |
| | (j) | ne pouvait (pas) manquer d'intéresser | 1 |
| | (k) | à la découverte du Nouveau Monde | 1 |
| | (l) | leurs aînés | 1 |

**Examiner's tip** (a) Did you remember to read the headings and sub-headings as well as the main body of the passage?

(f) *des aficionados* would probably be awarded a half-mark; it is not fully correct because it does not include the idea of **to** the fans as expressed in *aux enthousiastes*.

**G(ii)**

| 1 | 2 | 3 | 4 | 5 | 6 |
|---|---|---|---|---|---|
| (g) | (f) | (b) | (a) | (d) | (e) |

6

**Examiner's tip** This is a relatively easy 'matching definitions to statistics' exercise. The only one likely to cause any problems is **3**; at first sight there is no equivalent for the number **6**, but a closer investigation reveals that *parc Astérix* is about to open for its seventh season, therefore six have already been completed.

| Task | | Answer | Mark |
|------|------|--------|------|
| **H** | (a) | (parce qu'il) n'y avait pas de trains | 1 |
| | (b) | des centaines de personnes (or des SDF) (1); les bancs (1) | 2 |
| | (c) | rationnelle (or pas émotive) | 1 |
| | (d) | inconvénients | 1 |
| | (e) | normal | 1 |
| | (f) | facile à évaluer | 1 |
| | (g) | clochards | 1 |
| | (h) | chercher (or rencontrer) | 1 |
| | (i) | trois semaines (1); souffrir de pathologies considérables (1) | 2 |
| | (j) | moins | 1 |
| | (k) | par jour | 1 |
| | (l) | quatre | 1 |

| Task | Answer | Mark |
|------|--------|------|

At first sight this article looks difficult, particularly if you don't know what SDF stands for. Look closely at the first paragraph and you will find its meaning.

(a) It isn't possible to 'lift' directly from the passage here, because the construction is started for you. Think what the text means, then put it into your own words in French using the words you have been given as a starting point. *Pour cause de trafic nul* means 'because there were no trains'.

(c) Be careful: the text says *éviter de raisonner de manière émotive*, but the phrase you are given is more positive.

(e) This requires you to show your understanding of this section. The paragraph refers to the abnormal rhythm of life of those who live underground, so it follows that those who live above ground must have a more 'normal' rhythm.

(f) Again, you have to give the adjective **opposite** in meaning to the one in the passage, because the sentence is negative.

(g) *au bout de* means 'after'.

(i) Various possibilities are acceptable for the second gap; you should imply the destruction of mind rather than body.

(j) Read the question carefully. The passage tells you that those who live below ground suffer from *désocialisation* more quickly than those who live in the streets, but the sentence refers to the street dwellers.

(l) Did you realise that *la Régie* is the same as the *RATP* (*Régie Autonome des Transports Parisiens*)?

**I**

| 1 | 2 | 3 | 4 | 5 | 6 | 7 | 8 | 9 | 10 |
|----|----|----|----|----|----|----|----|----|----|
| (f) | (g) | (b) | (d) | (j) | (c) | (a) | (h) | (i) | (e) |

**10**

You are supposed to be giving the order of events as they happened, which is not necessarily the same as the order in the passage. If you do not read to the end of the passage before you start, you will not realise that the whole business began with the theft of Peuron's papers and that the man thought to be Michel Peuron and mentioned in the first column is in fact someone else entirely.

| | | | |
|---|---|---|---|
| **J** | **1** | L'Eurostar. | **1** |
| | **2** | Le taux de change est très favorable (1); le voyage est très facile (1). | **2** |
| | **3** | Du parfum (1), du saumon fumé (1), des complets (1). | **3** |
| | **4** | Aux musées (1) et aux galeries d'art (1). | **2** |
| | **5** | Au café-bar à Waterloo (1), les Français ont l'air beaucoup plus enjoués que les Anglais (1). | **2** |
| | **6** | Il n'aime pas les salaires (en livres sterling) des Britanniques. | **1** |

# Reading answers

| Task | Answer | Mark |
|------|--------|------|

**Examiner's tip**  **1** *Eurostar* is more precise; examiners might only award a half mark to *le train*.

**3** Make sure you read the whole text; if you write *tailleurs* (used for women's suits) this is not quite correct as later in the passage the author makes it clear that he is referring to men's clothes.

**4** *musée d'art* is a state-owned art gallery; *galerie* is privately owned. There are two points allocated and you have to make a distinction between museums and art galleries, so it's better to use both words.

**K**  Allow one mark for each of the sections indicated.

Canada is not a real country./ It is made up of two races,/ two nations and two territories./

The new Prime Minister of Quebec remains faithful/ to the ideals and to the facility of speech/ which have made him so popular/ with his fellow citizens./ On Monday, Lucien Bouchard,/ as had been expected/ succeeded Jacques Parizeau,/ the resigning head of government/ who had previously announced/ his retirement from political life./

Bouchard had been/ the main driving force behind the campaign/ in favour of a 'Yes' vote/ in the referendum on sovereignty for Quebec/ just lost on 30th October last/ by those who favoured sovereignty./ Introducing his government,/ he announced that his chief goal would be/ to clean up public finances,/ so that Quebec might one day/ gain independence/ on a solid financial and social basis./    **25**

**Examiner's tip**  Take care with the tenses in this passage; there are several changes.

**L(i)**  (in each case the elements identified for re-wording are shown)

(a) pratiquement deux mille réponses/sont parvenues/aux enquêteurs

ceux qui sont chargés de l'enquête ont reçu presque 2000 réponses    **3**

(b) les femmes et les personnes plus de 50 ans/étant/majoritaires

la plupart des gens qui ont répondu sont ou des femmes ou des gens qui ont dépassé la cinquantaine    **3**

(c) font apparaître/néanmoins/d'intéressantes/tendances

révèlent quand même des traits qui excitent l'intérêt    **4**

(d) dans la population/interrogée

parmi ceux qui ont rempli le questionnaire    **2**

(e) consultent/le même médecin généraliste/depuis 10 à 20 ans

continuent à consulter le médecin de famille qu'ils ont choisi il y a longtemps    **3**

| Task | Answer | Mark |
|------|--------|------|

**Examiner's tip**    (a)/(b) There is no need to change *deux mille* or *les femmes*.

(c) It's not easy to find another word for *tendances*, but *traits* expresses the idea if not the exact equivalent. Remember that you are being asked to show that you have understood.

(e) This, too, expresses the general meaning of the text. It will not always be easy to find alternatives, because the writer of the original text presumably chose the words that best expressed what he wanted to say.

**L(ii)**

(a) Three quarters thought that a doctor 'may' tell the family of a minor if he/she has AIDS (1), and over half thought that the doctor could do so in the case of an adult (1).    **2**

(b) 86% – those who ask the doctor to make a home visit during the day (1). 70% – those who ask him/her to make a home visit at the weekend (1).    **2**

(c) Gynaecologist (1), children's specialist (1), heart specialist (1).    **3**

(d) They can get a certificate entitling them to a voting proxy.    **1**

(e) Competence.    **1**

(f) That their doctor doesn't wash hands (1) before examining them (1).    **2**

(g) It's not a question of cutting down on medical care (1) but of improving the relationship (1) between quality and price (1).    **3**

(h) They should consider setting up a subscription system (1) and put the doctor in charge of his health budget (1) so that he would take care to prescribe useful medecines (1) and use hospitals and services that give good value for money (1).    **4**

**Examiner's tip**    Look for key words in the question and in the passage; use your dictionary sensibly. (e.g. AIDS = *sida*: this tells you where to look for your answer.

(a) If you have a comprehension question relating to percentages or statistics when there are several different figures close together, take care to relate the numbers to the correct 'definition'.

(h) Don't forget to answer 'and why?'.

**M(i)** 1    F    **1**

     2    V    **1**

     3    F    **1**

     4    F    **1**

     5    V    **1**

**Examiner's tip**    **1** The answer is in the subheading.

**3** Read right to the end of the sentences. Certainly *Déclic* is bringing together students and teachers, but for two sessions of three days each, which is not the same as five days.

*Letts*
Q&A

| Task | Answer | Mark |
|------|--------|------|

**4** This statement is correct except for the tense. The text says *sera créée* but the phrase in the exercise is *on vient de créer* (has just been set up).

**5** *l'objectif* is the same as *le but* (goal). Look for synonyms in this type of exercise.

| | | | |
|------|---|----------------------------------|---|
| **M(ii)** | **1** | concilier | 1 |
| | **2** | prochainement | 1 |
| | **3** | département | 1 |
| | **4** | l'enceinte | 1 |
| | **5** | reconduite | 1 |
| | **6** | s'achever (avec un succès réel) | 1 |
| | **7** | individualisme | 1 |

**Examiner's tip** These are basically dictionary definitions of the words as they are used in the context of the passage. Some Boards set this type of exercise, but others are more likely to ask you to find the equivalent of a whole phrase, not just a single word.

| | | | |
|------|---|----------------------------------|---|
| **M(iii)** | **1** | What is the daily life of university students like? | 1 |
| | **2** | A student association (1). Its President says that an association of any type needs to have been in existence for two years (1) for it to be fully effective (1). | 3 |
| | **3** | It's only at first degree level (1) that students leave home (1) and look for a room in town (1); others prefer to continue living at home (1) and spend a lot of time travelling because of it (1). | 5 |

| | | | |
|------|---|------------|---|
| **N(i)** | **1** | aller | 1 |
| | **2** | emprunter | 1 |
| | **3** | permettra | 1 |
| | **4** | conduisant | 1 |
| | **5** | suivez | 1 |
| | **6** | conduira | 1 |
| | **7** | racontera | 1 |
| | **8** | prenez | 1 |

**Examiner's tip** Notice that the sections of the text to which each part of the question refers are clearly stated.

This question is not as straightforward as it appears. As in the similar question in the Listening unit, the verbs in the list can be divided into several categories: infinitives, future tense (various endings), *vous* form of the present tense, and one present participle. A quick look at the text suggests that you will need to use the *vous* ending in **3**, **6** and **7**. It is not, in fact, correct in any of them (because in each case *vous* is not the subject of the verb) but you do need the *-ez* ending in **5** and **8** because the command form of the verb is required.

| Task | Answer | Mark |
|------|--------|------|

**1** After *pour* you are sure to need an infinitive.

**2** This construction also requires an infinitive.

**3** The subject of the verb is *celle qui* (see general note above)

**4** A present participle follows *en* ('by taking you')

**5** and **8** The command form of the verb is needed.

**6** The subject is *celle-ci*.

**7** Subject is *la Haute-Garonne.*

**N(ii)**

If you are romantic by nature/ you will probably prefer to follow the Garonne,/ crossing the region from north to south./ Or to follow the Route des Grands Espaces,/ from Saint Gaudens to Bourg d'Oueil near Bagnères-de-Luchon./ From undulating countryside/ to imposing mountains,/ open your eyes wide/and breathe deeply;/ mountains of dizzying height,/ leaping waterfalls,/ flocks of sheep/ led by an old shepherd,/ isolated villages./ It's another world you will discover;/ on foot, on horseback,/ by mountain bike, in a canoe;/ or maybe from higher still,/ by parapenting or hang-gliding,/ which are very popular in the Luchon region./

**20**

> **Examiner's tip**  On the whole it is safe to leave names – of people and places – in French (the obvious exceptions are places that have an English equivalent such as *Londres, Bruxelles, Bretagne, Douvres*). If you want to translate a place name, make sure that it gives the feel of the original (e.g. *Route des Grands Espaces* might be translated as the 'Route of wide-open spaces'; but the French is probably better in this case).
>
> The vocabulary in this section is specialised to some extent, being descriptive and even poetic in parts; but as a test it is valid even in the new syllabuses where a 'work-related task' might be to translate a brochure for a tourist area. You would, after all, have access to a dictionary.

**N(iii)**

découvrirez, vignes, faut, vendent, spécialités

**5**

> **Examiner's tip**  This *il* only makes sense if it is the impersonal 'it'. The last blank requires you to understand what *foie gras, confit* and *cassoulet* are, but this is reasonable as you should be studying the culture as well as the language. Gastronomy is very important to the French.

**O(i)**

Des gouvernements successifs en France/ ont eu tendance/ à voiler/ tant que possible/ le fait qu'il existe/ de graves problèmes d'ordre public./ Sans doute est-ce le cas/ en ce qui concerne la délinquance,/ la criminalité même,/ dans les écoles;/ personne n'a voulu en parler./ Les directeurs,/ ayant peur/ des conséquences éventuelles,/ ont constaté que/ ce n'est pas la peine/ d'en faire un drame./ On a persuadé/ les parents des victimes/ de ne pas se plaindre./ En 1990 certains journaux disaient même/ que les élèves qui manifestaient dans les rues/ en réclamant/ davantage de surveillants/ étaient motivés par le racisme./

**25**

| Task | Answer | Mark |
|------|--------|------|

**O(ii)**  (a)  La misère (**or** des raisons économiques) (1); il est plus facile d'être criminel (1) que de faire des études à l'école (1). **3**

(b)  On ne fait rien pour combattre le crime. **1**

(c)  Combattre les conséquences (1); en traiter les causes sociales (1). **2**

(d)  Un professeur a constaté qu'il était content qu'un élève l'ait frappé (1) parce que de cet incident est né une sorte de communication entre les deux (1). **2**

**O(iii)** 1  (b)

2  (c)

3  (c)

4  (a)

5  (b) **5**